Collins

PRACTICE MULTIPLE CHOICE QUESTIONS

CSEC®
Integrated
Science

T0364566

Anne Tindale & Peter DeFreitas

Collins

William Collins' dream of knowledge for all began with the publication of his first book in 1819.
A self-educated mill worker, he not only enriched millions of lives, but also founded a flourishing publishing house.
Today, staying true to this spirit, Collins books are packed with inspiration, innovation and practical expertise.
They place you at the centre of a world of possibility and give you exactly what you need to explore it.

Collins. Freedom to teach.

Published by Collins
An imprint of HarperCollins*Publishers*
The News Building
1 London Bridge Street
London
SE1 9GF

Browse the complete Collins Caribbean catalogue at
www.collins.co.uk/caribbeanschools

HarperCollins*Publishers*
Macken House, 39/40 Mayor Street Upper
Dublin 1, D01 C9W8, Ireland

10 9 8 7 6 5

978-0-00-835977-5

Collins CSEC® Integrated Science Multiple Choice Practice is an independent publication and has not been authorised, sponsored or otherwise approved by **CXC®**.

CSEC® is a registered trademark of the **Caribbean Examinations Council (CXC®)**.

British Library Cataloguing in Publication Data

A catalogue record for this publication is available from the British Library.

The publishers gratefully acknowledge the permission granted to reproduce the copyright material in this book. Every effort has been made to trace copyright holders and to obtain their permission for the use of copyright material. The publishers will gladly receive any information enabling them to rectify any error or omission at the first opportunity.

Authors: Anne Tindale and Peter DeFreitas
Reviewer: Shaun deSouza
Publisher: Dr Elaine Higgleton
Commissioning editor: Tom Hardy
Project lead: Julianna Dunn
Copy editor: Aidan Gill
Proofreader: Helen Bleck
Illustrator: Ann Paganuzzi
Production controller: Lyndsey Rogers
Typesetter: QBS Learning
Cover designers: Kevin Robbins and Gordon MacGilp

Printed and bound in the UK using 100% Renewable Electricity at CPI Group (UK) Ltd

This book is produced from independently certified FSC™ paper to ensure responsible forest management.
For more information visit: www.harpercollins.co.uk/green

Contents

Download answers for free at www.collins.co.uk/caribbeanschools

Structure of the CSEC® Integrated Science Paper 1 Examination

There are **60 questions**, known as **items**, in the Paper 1 examination and the duration of the examination is **1¼ hours**. The paper is worth **30%** of your final examination mark.

The table below gives the approximate number of questions from each section of the syllabus.

Section	*Approximate* **Number of Questions**
A: The Organism and Its Environment	24
B: The Home and Workplace	20
C: Earth's Place in the Universe	16
Total	**60**

The questions test one profile, **knowledge and comprehension**. Questions will be presented in a variety of ways including the use of diagrams, tables, data, graphs, prose or other stimulus material.

Each question is allocated 1 mark. You will not lose a mark if a question is answered incorrectly.

Examination Tips

General strategies for answering multiple choice questions

- Read every word of each question very carefully and make sure you understand exactly what it is asking. Even if you think that the question appears simple or straightforward there may be important information you could easily miss, especially small but very important words, such as *all* or *only*.

- When faced with a question that seems unfamiliar, read it very carefully. Underline or circle the key pieces of information provided. Re-read it if necessary to make sure you are very clear as to what it is asking and that you are not misinterpreting it.

- Each question has four options, **(A)**, **(B)**, **(C)** and **(D)**, and only one is the correct answer. Look at all the options very carefully as the differences between them may be very subtle; never stop when you come across an option you think is the one required. Cross out options that you know are incorrect for certain. There may be two options that appear very similar; identify the difference between the two so you can select the correct answer.

- You have approximately 1¼ minutes per question. Some questions can be answered in less than 1 minute while other questions may require longer because of the reasoning or calculation involved. Do not spend too long on any one question.

- If a question appears difficult place a mark, such as an asterisk, on your answer sheet beside the question number and return to it when you have finished answering all the other questions. Remember to carefully remove the asterisk, or other markings, from the answer sheet using a good clean eraser as soon as you have completed the question.

- Answer every question. Marks are not deducted for incorrect answers. Therefore, it is in your best interest to make an educated guess in instances where you do not know the answer. Never leave a question unanswered.

- Always ensure that you are shading the correct question number on your answer sheet. It is very easy to make a mistake, especially if you plan on returning to skipped questions.

- Some questions may ask which of the options is NOT correct or is INCORRECT, or they may state that all options are correct EXCEPT. Pay close attention to these questions because it is easy to fail to see these key words and so answer the questions incorrectly.

- When answering a question that asks which option is NOT correct, is INCORRECT or that uses the word EXCEPT, place a T or an F next to each option to indicate if it is true or false. The correct answer to the question is the one with the *F*.

- Some questions may give two or more answers that could be correct and you are asked to determine which is the BEST or MOST LIKELY. You must consider each answer very carefully before making your choice because the differences between them may be very subtle.

- When a question gives three or four answers numbered **I**, **II** and **III** or **I**, **II**, **III** and **IV**, one or more of these answers may be correct. You will then be given four combinations as options, for example:

  (A) I only

  (B) I and II only

  (C) II and III only

  (D) I, II and III

  Place a tick by all the answers that you think are correct before you decide on the final correct combination.

- Do not make any assumptions about your choice of options. Just because two answers in succession have been **C**, it does not mean that the next one cannot be **C** as well.

- Try to leave time at the end of the examination to check over your answers, but never change an answer until you have thought about it again very carefully.

Strategies for the CSEC® Integrated Science Paper 1

- Non-programmable calculators are allowed in the examination; however, when you use your calculator, always recheck your answer since it is easy to press the wrong key.

- If the question requires recall of a simple fact, such as the name of a labelled structure in a diagram, a piece of apparatus, a chemical substance or a process, it is better to try to work out the answer before looking at the options given. Looking at the answers first could influence your choice and you may select an incorrect answer.

- When answering a question about a labelled diagram, make sure you know exactly which structure each label line is indicating before answering.

- Questions are taken from all areas of the syllabus for the multiple choice examination, and the examination focuses on detail. Make sure you cover the entire syllabus and learn all the facts, however small, that you have been taught.

- It is extremely important that you can readily recall each mathematical equation listed in the Summary of Equations Used in This Book on page vi.

Summary of Equations Used in This Book

Worded equations	Symbolic equations
work = force × distance moved in direction of force	$W = F \times d$
energy = force × distance moved in direction of force	$E = F \times d$
$\text{power} = \dfrac{\text{work}}{\text{time}}$ or $\text{power} = \dfrac{\text{energy}}{\text{time}}$	$P = \dfrac{W}{t}$ or $P = \dfrac{E}{t}$
momentum = mass × velocity	$p = m \times v$
voltage = current × resistance	$V = I \times R$
power = voltage × current	$P = V \times I$
$\text{mechanical advantage} = \dfrac{\text{load}}{\text{effort}}$	$MA = \dfrac{L}{E}$
$\text{efficiency} = \dfrac{\text{useful energy output}}{\text{energy input}} \times 100\%$	$\eta = \dfrac{\text{useful } E_{out}}{E_{in}} \times 100\%$
$\text{efficiency} = \dfrac{\text{load} \times \text{distance moved by load}}{\text{effort} \times \text{distance moved by effort}} \times 100\%$	$\eta = \dfrac{L \times d_L}{E \times d_E} \times 100\%$
$\text{density} = \dfrac{\text{mass}}{\text{volume}}$	$\rho = \dfrac{m}{V}$
force = mass × acceleration	$F = m \times a$
weight = mass × acceleration due to gravity	$w = m \times g$

Negative exponent method:

This book uses negative exponents instead of slashes to indicate division of units.

Use of slash	Use of negative exponent
m/s	m s^{-1}
m/s^2	m s^{-2}

1 Which of the following statements is correct?

(A) A liquid takes the shape of the container it is in.   (A)

(B) A gas has a definite shape.   (B)

(C) A plasma can conduct an electric current.   (C)

(D) The volume of a solid is variable.   (D)

2 Compared to the particles in liquids, the particles in solids

(A) have more space between them   (A)

(B) move faster   (B)

(C) have less kinetic energy   (C)

(D) have weaker forces of attraction between them   (D)

3 Changing a solid to a liquid is known as

(A) melting   (A)

(B) dissolving   (B)

(C) solidifying   (C)

(D) boiling   (D)

4 The melting and boiling points of four substances are given in the table below. Which substance will be a gas at room temperature?

	Substance	Melting point/°C	Boiling point/°C	
(A)	I	91	213	(A)
(B)	II	−163	−4	(B)
(C)	III	−65	87	(C)
(D)	IV	316	543	(D)

5 Which of the following BEST describes what happens to particles when a liquid freezes?

(A) They gain kinetic energy and lose freedom of movement. Ⓐ

(B) They lose kinetic energy and lose freedom of movement. Ⓑ

(C) They lose kinetic energy and become more spread out. Ⓒ

(D) They gain kinetic energy and become more ordered. Ⓓ

Items **6–7** refer to the following diagram of an animal cell.

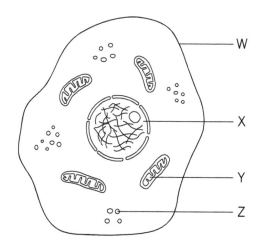

6 The structure labelled Y is a

(A) ribosome Ⓐ

(B) chloroplast Ⓑ

(C) vacuole Ⓒ

(D) mitochondrion Ⓓ

7 When this is removed, the cell is unable to divide.

(A) W Ⓐ

(B) X Ⓑ

(C) Y Ⓒ

(D) Z Ⓓ

Items **8–9** refer to the following cellular structures:

(A) chromosomes

(B) cytoplasm

(C) chloroplasts

(D) ribosomes

Match EACH item below with one of the options above. Each option may be used once, more than once or not at all.

8 Contain(s) genetic information.

(A) ⒜

(B) ⒝

(C) ⒞

(D) ⒟

9 Where proteins are synthesised.

(A) ⒜

(B) ⒝

(C) ⒞

(D) ⒟

10 Which option in the table below is INCORRECT?

	Typical plant cell	Typical animal cell	
(A)	has a cell wall	has no cell wall	⒜
(B)	has one large vacuole	has many small vacuoles	⒝
(C)	contains chloroplasts	has no chloroplasts	⒞
(D)	has no mitochondria	contains mitochondria	⒟

11 Which of the following statements about microbes is INCORRECT?

(A) Viruses and bacteria are classified as microbes. (A)

(B) Useful drugs can be produced by certain microbes. (B)

(C) All microbes cause disease. (C)

(D) Some microbes cause food to spoil. (D)

12 Microbes have the following positive effects.

   I They recycle nutrients from waste matter.

   II They decompose food.

   III They decompose sewage.

   IV They fix nitrogen from the atmosphere.

(A) I and III only (A)

(B) II and IV only (B)

(C) I, II and III only (C)

(D) I, III and IV only (D)

13 Which of the following BEST describes what happens during osmosis?

(A) Molecules move from a dilute solution to a more concentrated solution through a partially permeable membrane. (A)

(B) Water molecules diffuse from a dilute solution to a concentrated solution. (B)

(C) Water molecules move through a partially permeable membrane from a dilute solution to a concentrated solution. (C)

(D) Water molecules diffuse from a concentrated solution to a dilute solution through a partially permeable membrane. (D)

14 Which of the following cell structures is/are partially permeable?

    I The cell membrane

    II The cell wall

    III The cytoplasm

(A) I only   (A)

(B) II only   (B)

(C) I and III only   (C)

(D) I, II and III   (D)

15 Diffusion is important to living organisms to

    I obtain oxygen for respiration

    II get rid of carbon dioxide produced in photosynthesis

    III obtain water for photosynthesis

(A) I only   (A)

(B) I and III only   (B)

(C) II and III only   (C)

(D) I, II and III   (D)

16 Which of the following correctly summarises the importance of osmosis and active transport in living organisms?

	Osmosis	**Active transport**	
(A)	helps leaves obtain water for photosynthesis	means by which roots of plants absorb mineral ions	(A)
(B)	means by which cells take in water	means by which leaves absorb oxygen	(B)
(C)	means by which water vapour passes out of leaves	helps absorb glucose in the ileum	(C)
(D)	helps non-woody stems stand erect	means by which carbon dioxide moves out of cells	(D)

1 Which of the following options correctly compares sexual and asexual reproduction?

	Sexual reproduction	Asexual reproduction	
(A)	a rapid process	a slow process	Ⓐ
(B)	involves one parent	involves two parents	Ⓑ
(C)	produces offspring that are genetically non-identical	produces offspring that are genetically identical	Ⓒ
(D)	does not require the fusion of gametes	requires the fusion of gametes	Ⓓ

2 Which of the following is/are advantages of asexual reproduction?

I It enables population sizes to increase rapidly.

II It maintains undesirable characteristics within populations.

III It enables species to evolve.

(A) I only   Ⓐ

(B) I and III only   Ⓑ

(C) II and III only   Ⓒ

(D) I, II and III only   Ⓓ

Items **3–4** refer to the following methods of asexual reproduction:

(A) cuttings

(B) budding

(C) runners

(D) tissue culture

Match EACH item below with one of the options on the previous page. Each option may be used once, more than once or not at all.

3 Which method would be MOST suitable for a gardener to use to propagate hibiscus plants?

(A)   Ⓐ

(B)   Ⓑ

(C)   Ⓒ

(D)   Ⓓ

4 The initial stage of the method requires sterile conditions.

(A)   Ⓐ

(B)   Ⓑ

(C)   Ⓒ

(D)   Ⓓ

Items **5–6** refer to the following section through a flower.

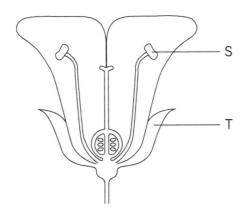

5 The structure labelled S is the

(A) style   Ⓐ

(B) anther   Ⓑ

(C) stigma   Ⓒ

(D) filament   Ⓓ

6 What is the main function of the structure labelled T?

(A) To protect the petals. Ⓐ

(B) To protect the flower before it opens. Ⓑ

(C) To attract bees for pollination. Ⓒ

(D) To surround and support the other parts of the flower. Ⓓ

7 Which of the following BEST describes pollination?

(A) Production of pollen grains by the anthers. Ⓐ

(B) Production of pollen grains by the stigma. Ⓑ

(C) Transfer of pollen grains from stigmas to anthers. Ⓒ

(D) Transfer of pollen grains from anthers to stigmas. Ⓓ

8 Which of the following are important advantages of cross-pollination over self-pollination?

I Some offspring produced in cross-pollination may have inferior characteristics to both parents.

II Cross-pollination leads to greater variation within the offspring.

III Bees are never needed for cross-pollination.

IV The seeds produced by cross-pollination are more likely to germinate.

(A) I and II only Ⓐ

(B) I and III only Ⓑ

(C) II and IV only Ⓒ

(D) II, III and IV only Ⓓ

9 Which of the following events does NOT take place after pollination in a mango flower ?

(A) The ovule develops into the seed.   Ⓐ

(B) The pollen grain travels down the style.   Ⓑ

(C) The ovary develops into the fruit.   Ⓒ

(D) The male and female gametes fuse.   Ⓓ

Items **10–11** refer to the following diagram of the human female reproductive system.

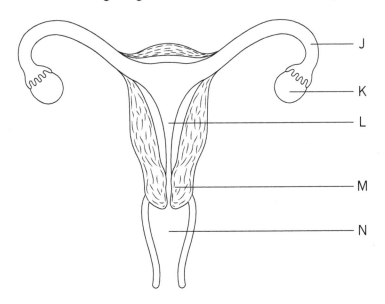

10 The structure labelled M is the

(A) uterus   Ⓐ

(B) vagina   Ⓑ

(C) ovary   Ⓒ

(D) cervix   Ⓓ

11 Where fertilisation occurs.

(A) J   Ⓐ

(B) K   Ⓑ

(C) L   Ⓒ

(D) N   Ⓓ

Item **12** refers to the following diagram of the male reproductive system.

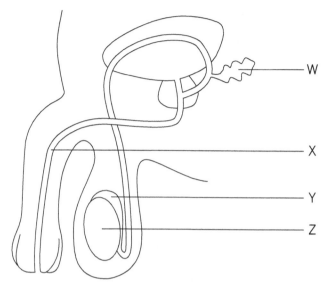

12 Which option correctly matches the labelled structure with its functions?

	Contributes to the production of semen	Stores sperm	
(A)	W	Y	Ⓐ
(B)	W	Z	Ⓑ
(C)	Z	W	Ⓒ
(D)	X	Y	Ⓓ

13 Which of the following correctly summarises the pathway along which sperm travels?

(A) testis ⟶ sperm duct ⟶ prostate gland ⟶ urethra   Ⓐ

(B) testis ⟶ epididymis ⟶ sperm duct ⟶ ureter   Ⓑ

(C) epididymis ⟶ sperm duct ⟶ prostate gland ⟶ urethra   Ⓒ

(D) testis ⟶ epididymis ⟶ sperm duct ⟶ urethra   Ⓓ

14 The diagram below shows how the uterus lining changes during the menstrual cycle. Which point indicates the state of the uterus lining when ovulation is MOST likely to occur?

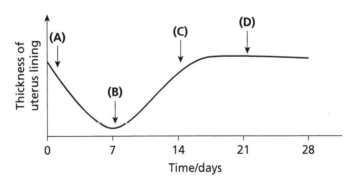

(A) Ⓐ

(B) Ⓑ

(C) Ⓒ

(D) Ⓓ

15 Which of the following options is correct?

	Hormone	Secreted by	Function	
(A)	oestrogen	primary follicle	stimulates the uterus lining to thicken	Ⓐ
(B)	oestrogen	Graafian follicle	maintains a thickened uterus lining	Ⓑ
(C)	progesterone	Graafian follicle	stimulates the uterus lining to break down	Ⓒ
(D)	progesterone	corpus luteum	maintains a thickened uterus lining	Ⓓ

16 During menopause

    I a female can no longer become pregnant

    II the secretion of oestrogen increases

    III menstruation stops

(A) I only   Ⓐ

(B) I and III only   Ⓑ

(C) II and III only   Ⓒ

(D) I, II and III   Ⓓ

17 The following events take place between conception and birth.

P   The placenta develops.

Q   The pituitary gland secretes oxytocin.

R   The embryo sinks into the uterus lining.

S   The cervix dilates.

The correct order of events is

(A) R, P, Q, S   Ⓐ

(B) Q, R, S, P   Ⓑ

(C) R, Q, P, S   Ⓒ

(D) P, R, S, Q   Ⓓ

Item **18** refers to the following diagram of a human foetus in the uterus.

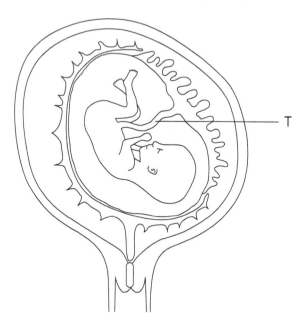

18 The structure labelled T is the

    (**A**) amnion   Ⓐ

    (**B**) umbilical cord   Ⓑ

    (**C**) ileum   Ⓒ

    (**D**) placenta   Ⓓ

19 Which of the following is NOT a function of the placenta?

    (**A**) To secrete progesterone.   Ⓐ

    (**B**) To obtain oxygen from the mother for the foetus.   Ⓑ

    (**C**) To produce food for the developing foetus.   Ⓒ

    (**D**) To remove carbon dioxide from the developing foetus.   Ⓓ

Items **20–21** refer to the following birth control methods:

    (**A**) withdrawal

    (**B**) contraceptive pill

    (**C**) vasectomy

    (**D**) diaphragm

Match EACH item below with one of the options above. Each option may be used once, more than once or not at all.

20 Which method makes use of hormones to prevent pregnancy from occurring?

    (**A**)   Ⓐ

    (**B**)   Ⓑ

    (**C**)   Ⓒ

    (**D**)   Ⓓ

21 Which is the MOST unreliable method?

    (**A**)   Ⓐ

    (**B**)   Ⓑ

    (**C**)   Ⓒ

    (**D**)   Ⓓ

22 The MAIN advantage of using condoms as contraceptive devices over other contraceptives is that they

(A) are easy to use   (A)

(B) are readily available   (B)

(C) are reliable   (C)

(D) protect against sexually transmitted infections   (D)

23 Which of the following statements is correct?

(A) When pregnant, a woman must protect herself against harmful high-frequency sound waves produced by ultrasound scans.   (A)

(B) A pregnant woman should eat a balanced diet which is high in fats and carbohydrates throughout her pregnancy.   (B)

(C) A pregnant woman should avoid doing any exercise to ensure she does not have a miscarriage.   (C)

(D) When pregnant, a woman should visit her doctor regularly.   (D)

24 Which of the following statements is NOT true about breast milk?

(A) It contains antibodies from the mother.   (A)

(B) It increases the baby's risk of developing asthma if the mother has asthma.   (B)

(C) It is sterile.   (C)

(D) It contains the correct proportions of all the nutrients the baby needs.   (D)

25 An immunisation programme within a country should effectively control the spread of which STI within that country?

(A) Gonorrhoea   (A)

(B) Hepatitis B   (B)

(C) HIV/AIDS   (C)

(D) Genital herpes   (D)

26 Which of the following sexually transmitted infections is/are caused by a bacterium?

    I herpes

    II gonorrhoea

    III syphilis

(A) II only   Ⓐ

(B) I and III only   Ⓑ

(C) II and III only   Ⓒ

(D) I, II and III   Ⓓ

27 Which option correctly matches the sexually transmitted infection with some of its main symptoms?

	Infection	Symptoms	
(A)	syphilis	painless genital sores and a red, non-itchy body rash	Ⓐ
(B)	hepatitis B	pain or burning sensation when urinating and swollen glands	Ⓑ
(C)	genital herpes	dark coloured urine and jaundice of the skin	Ⓒ
(D)	gonorrhoea	flu-like symptoms and blisters on the genitals	Ⓓ

28 Which of the following statements is INCORRECT?

(A) Candida can be treated with antifungal tablets.   Ⓐ

(B) Hepatitis B can lead to serious liver damage.   Ⓑ

(C) The spread of HIV/AIDS can be controlled by setting up immunisation programmes.   Ⓒ

(D) Genital herpes cannot be cured.   Ⓓ

29 The spread of gonorrhoea can be controlled by

      I using condoms during sexual intercourse

      II implementing needle and syringe exchange programmes for drug addicts

      III setting up education programmes

(A) I only   Ⓐ

(B) II only   Ⓑ

(C) I and III only   Ⓒ

(D) I, II and III   Ⓓ

30 The following table gives the average length of 10 hibiscus leaves, growing on the same plant, measured at 4-day intervals for 36 days.

Time/days	0	4	8	12	16	20	24	28	32	36
Average length of leaves/mm	5	12	36	62	76	83	87	89	90	90

What shape is the growth curve for the leaves?

(A) A straight line at 45° to the x-axis.   Ⓐ

(B) A straight line parallel to the x-axis.   Ⓑ

(C) Bell-shaped.   Ⓒ

(D) S-shaped.   Ⓓ

Items **31–32** refer to the following diagram of a bean seed.

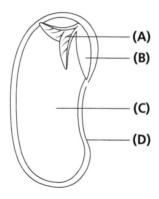

31 Which part of the seed will grow into the root system?

(A)   Ⓐ

(B)   Ⓑ

(C)   Ⓒ

(D)   Ⓓ

32 Where is protein MOST likely to be stored?

(A)   Ⓐ

(B)   Ⓑ

(C)   Ⓒ

(D)   Ⓓ

33 The growth of the human population is currently at which point on the growth curve illustrated below?

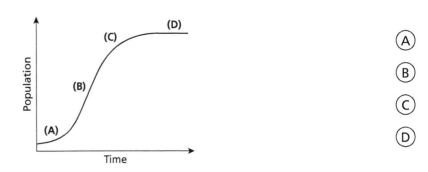

Ⓐ

Ⓑ

Ⓒ

Ⓓ

34 Which of the following statements is/are true?

   I Birth control can help reduce human population growth.

   II Teenage pregnancy has very little effect on the growth of the human population.

   III If the human population continues to grow, overall living standards should improve.

(A) I only   Ⓐ

(B) I and III only   Ⓑ

(C) II and III only   Ⓒ

(D) I, II and III   Ⓓ

A3: Food and Nutrition

1 The substrates needed for photosynthesis include

    I water

    II carbon dioxide

    III chlorophyll

(A) III only   Ⓐ

(B) I and II only   Ⓑ

(C) II and III only   Ⓒ

(D) I, II and III   Ⓓ

2 Which of the following chemical equations MOST accurately summarises the process of photosynthesis?

(A) $CO_2 + H_2O \xrightarrow{\text{light energy}} C_6H_{12}O_6 + O_2$ Ⓐ

(B) $6CO_2 + 6H_2O \longrightarrow C_6H_{12}O_6 + 6O_2$ Ⓑ

(C) $6CO_2 + 6H_2O \xrightarrow{\text{light energy}} C_{12}H_{22}O_{11} + 6O_2$ Ⓒ

(D) $6CO_2 + 6H_2O \xrightarrow{\text{light energy}} C_6H_{12}O_6 + 6O_2$ Ⓓ

3 Which reagent would be the BEST to test a hibiscus leaf to see if it has been photosynthesising?

(A) Benedict's solution   Ⓐ

(B) biuret solution   Ⓑ

(C) ethanol   Ⓒ

(D) iodine solution   Ⓓ

4 During photosynthesis, light energy is converted into

   (A) heat energy   Ⓐ

   (B) electrical energy   Ⓑ

   (C) chemical energy   Ⓒ

   (D) kinetic energy   Ⓓ

5 A farmer wishes to grow maize on the side of a hill, and a gardener wishes to grow sweet peppers, but he has very little space available. Which option gives the MOST suitable method for each to use?

	Method most suitable for the farmer	Method most suitable for the gardener	
(A)	contour ploughing	greenhouse farming	Ⓐ
(B)	organic farming	strip planting	Ⓑ
(C)	contour ploughing	container gardening	Ⓒ
(D)	strip planting	greenhouse farming	Ⓓ

6 Which of the following statements is INCORRECT?

   (A) Organic farming uses synthetic pesticides.   Ⓐ

   (B) Growing crops using hydroponics ensures that they will not be damaged by soil-borne pests.   Ⓑ

   (C) Soil is less likely to erode when crops are grown on terraces.   Ⓒ

   (D) Tissue culture can be used to produce crops with desirable characteristics.   Ⓓ

7 Which of the following BEST describes an ecosystem?

   (A) A community of living organisms interacting with each other and with their physical environment.   Ⓐ

   (B) All the members of a species living together in a particular place.   Ⓑ

   (C) The place where an organism lives.   Ⓒ

   (D) Many populations of different species living together in a particular area and interacting with each other.   Ⓓ

8 Which of the following statements is correct?

(A) Green plants are omnivores. Ⓐ

(B) A secondary consumer always feeds on a producer. Ⓑ

(C) Most primary consumers are herbivores. Ⓒ

(D) A food chain always begins with a decomposer. Ⓓ

9 Mosquito larvae are known to feed on microscopic algae. In a freshwater pond, egrets were seen catching the tilapia, and it is also known that tilapia feed on mosquito larvae. The correct food chain for the organisms in the pond is

(A) microscopic algae ⟶ tilapia ⟶ mosquito larvae ⟶ egrets Ⓐ

(B) egrets ⟶ tilapia ⟶ mosquito larvae ⟶ microscopic algae Ⓑ

(C) mosquito larvae ⟶ microscopic algae ⟶ tilapia ⟶ egrets Ⓒ

(D) microscopic algae ⟶ mosquito larvae ⟶ tilapia ⟶ egrets Ⓓ

10 The table below gives the food sources of several animal species in a marine ecosystem.

Animal	Food source(s)
sea turtle	jellyfish and crabs
zooplankton	plant plankton
crab	shrimp
jellyfish	zooplankton
shrimp	plant plankton

Which of following statements is INCORRECT?

(A) Shrimp are primary consumers. Ⓐ

(B) Plant plankton are producers. Ⓑ

(C) Jellyfish are carnivores. Ⓒ

(D) Zooplankton are secondary consumers. Ⓓ

11 Decomposers

      I are macroorganisms

      II return minerals to the environment

      III feed on waste organic matter

(A) I only   Ⓐ

(B) I and III only   Ⓑ

(C) II and III only   Ⓒ

(D) I, II and III   Ⓓ

12 Which option correctly matches the food group with the MAIN nutrient that it supplies in the human diet?

	Food group	Main nutrient supplied	
(A)	non-starchy vegetables	carbohydrates	Ⓐ
(B)	fruits	protein	Ⓑ
(C)	staple foods	fat	Ⓒ
(D)	food from animals	protein	Ⓓ

13 Protein is needed in the human diet

      I for growth and repair of tissues

      II for storage

      III to make enzymes

      IV for insulation

(A) I and III only   Ⓐ

(B) II and IV only   Ⓑ

(C) I, II and III only   Ⓒ

(D) I, III and IV only   Ⓓ

14 The following table gives the energy requirements of four people. Two people are office workers of different genders and one is a professional footballer. Which person is MOST likely to be the male office worker?

	Person	Age/years	Energy requirements/kJ per day	
(A)	W	12	7 500	Ⓐ
(B)	X	25	8 500	Ⓑ
(C)	Y	25	10 000	Ⓒ
(D)	Z	25	12 500	Ⓓ

15 Which of the following statements is INCORRECT?

(A) Kwashiorkor is caused by a severe shortage of protein in the diet.   Ⓐ

(B) Food additives are harmless chemicals added to food to enhance its flavour or colour.   Ⓑ

(C) Consumption of excess protein in the diet causes the diet to be unbalanced.   Ⓒ

(D) A deficiency of vitamin D in the diet can lead to rickets.   Ⓓ

16 The following table shows the main constituents of four foods of equal mass. Which food would be LEAST suitable for a person with obesity?

	Food	Carbohydrate/g	Fat/g	Protein/g	Calcium/mg	Vitamin C/mg	
(A)	P	5	32	21	450	–	Ⓐ
(B)	Q	45	2	15	10	95	Ⓑ
(C)	R	24	95	5	150	5	Ⓒ
(D)	S	15	4	60	85	15	Ⓓ

17 A person suffering from anaemia should increase the consumption of foods rich in

(A) vitamin A   (A)

(B) vitamin B_1 (B)

(C) calcium   (C)

(D) iron   (D)

18 Three food items, T, U and V, were each crushed with 2 cm^3 of water and tested with the reagents shown in the table below.

Test solution	Resultant colour		
	T	U	V
Benedict's solution	orange	blue	blue
biuret solution	purple	purple	blue
iodine solution	orange-brown	orange-brown	blue-black

Which of the following statements is correct?

(A) T contained reducing sugars and starch.   (A)

(B) U was the only food item that contained protein.   (B)

(C) U contained reducing sugars as well as protein.   (C)

(D) V contained starch only.   (D)

19 Which of the following microorganisms can cause food to spoil?

     I viruses

     II bacteria

     III fungi

(A) I only   (A)

(B) I and II only   (B)

(C) II and III only   (C)

(D) I, II and III   (D)

20 The growth of bread mould can be slowed or prevented by

     I keeping the bread in a refrigerator

     II freezing the bread

     III storing the bread in a paper bag on a kitchen shelf

(A) II only   Ⓐ

(B) I and II only   Ⓑ

(C) I and III only   Ⓒ

(D) I, II and III   Ⓓ

Items **21–22** refer to the following methods of preserving food:

(A) salting

(B) pickling

(C) refrigeration

(D) pasteurisation

Match EACH item below with one of the options above. Each option may be used once, more than once or not at all.

21 Lowers the pH of the food, which prevents microorganisms from growing.

(A)   Ⓐ

(B)   Ⓑ

(C)   Ⓒ

(D)   Ⓓ

22 Creates unfavourable conditions for microorganisms by withdrawing water from the food.

(A)   (A)

(B)   (B)

(C)   (C)

(D)   (D)

23 Teeth are important in the process of digestion because they

      I turn insoluble food into soluble food

      II break down large food molecules to smaller molecules

      III increase the surface area of pieces of food

(A) I only   (A)

(B) III only   (B)

(C) II and III only   (C)

(D) I, II and III   (D)

24 Four different types of teeth are shown below.

Which of the following options correctly matches the tooth with its type and function?

	Tooth	Type	Function	
(A)	L	canine	tears food	(A)
(B)	M	molar	crushes food	(B)
(C)	N	incisor	grips food	(C)
(D)	O	premolar	cuts food	(D)

Item **25** refers to the following section through a tooth.

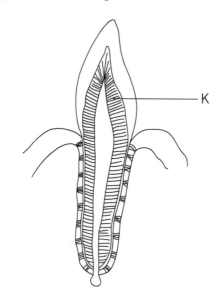

25 Structure K is the

(A) pulp cavity   Ⓐ

(B) dentine   Ⓑ

(C) enamel   Ⓒ

(D) cement   Ⓓ

26 Which of the following do NOT help to reduce tooth decay?

    I using dental floss daily

    II visiting a doctor regularly

    III eating sugary foods

    IV brushing teeth twice a day

(A) III only   Ⓐ

(B) I and IV only   Ⓑ

(C) II and III only   Ⓒ

(D) I, II and IV only   Ⓓ

Items **27–28** refer to the following diagram of the human alimentary canal.

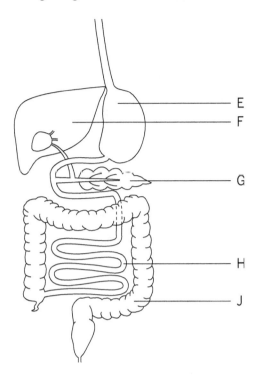

27 Which structure produces three different enzymes that digest proteins, lipids and starch?

(A) E   (A)

(B) F   (B)

(C) G   (C)

(D) H   (D)

28 Structure J is the

(A) colon   (A)

(B) ileum   (B)

(C) duodenum   (C)

(D) oesophagus   (D)

29 Which option correctly matches the enzyme with its digestion product(s)?

	Enzyme	Digestion product	
(A)	pepsin	amino acids	Ⓐ
(B)	salivary amylase	glucose	Ⓑ
(C)	lactase	lactose	Ⓒ
(D)	pancreatic lipase	fatty acids and glycerol	Ⓓ

30 People who have their gall bladders removed are MOST likely to have to avoid eating

(A) mangoes   Ⓐ

(B) boiled sweet potatoes   Ⓑ

(C) tomatoes   Ⓒ

(D) fried bacon   Ⓓ

31 Which of the following enzymes is responsible for completing the digestion of proteins?

(A) erepsin (peptidase)   Ⓐ

(B) pepsin   Ⓑ

(C) sucrase   Ⓒ

(D) trypsin   Ⓓ

32 Which of the following statements is INCORRECT?

(A) Both water and mineral salts can be absorbed from undigested food in the colon.   Ⓐ

(B) Egestion is the process by which the body uses the products of digestion.   Ⓑ

(C) Excess glucose produced in digestion can be converted into glycogen by liver cells.   Ⓒ

(D) Amino acids produced in digestion can be used to make enzymes.   Ⓓ

1. Multicellular organisms have developed transport systems because

   (A) they have a large surface area Ⓐ

   (B) they have a small surface area to volume ratio Ⓑ

   (C) their bodies are large enough to accommodate transport systems Ⓒ

   (D) they have a large surface area to volume ratio Ⓓ

2. Which of the following lists consists of substances that are transported around the bodies of plants?

   (A) oxygen, water, minerals, amino acids Ⓐ

   (B) sucrose, amino acids, water, minerals Ⓑ

   (C) carbon dioxide, water, glucose, minerals Ⓒ

   (D) amino acids, oxygen, sucrose, carbon dioxide Ⓓ

3. Which of the following statements is correct?

   (A) Xylem vessels transport water from the leaves of plants to their roots. Ⓐ

   (B) Phloem tissue transports mineral salts from the roots of plants to their leaves. Ⓑ

   (C) Food produced by the leaves of plants is transported to the fruits in phloem sieve tubes. Ⓒ

   (D) Dissolved oxygen is transported from the leaves of plants to the roots in xylem vessels. Ⓓ

4. Transpiration is BEST described as

   (A) the stream of water moving from roots to leaves Ⓐ

   (B) the movement of water through the stomata of leaves Ⓑ

   (C) the exchange of water vapour through the stomata of leaves Ⓒ

   (D) the loss of water vapour from leaves Ⓓ

5 Movement of water through a plant involves

    I capillary action

    II osmosis

    III active transport

(A) II only   Ⓐ

(B) I and II only   Ⓑ

(C) I and III only   Ⓒ

(D) I, II and III   Ⓓ

6 The following are characteristics of red blood cells, EXCEPT

(A) they are made in red bone marrow   Ⓐ

(B) they contain haemoglobin   Ⓑ

(C) they are discus-shaped   Ⓒ

(D) they are unable to reproduce   Ⓓ

<u>Items 7–8</u> refer to the following diagram, which shows cells found in human blood.

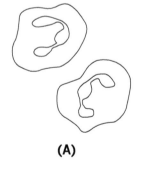 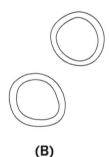 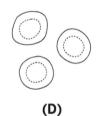

      (A)   **(B)**   **(C)**   **(D)**

7 Which cells are needed to help blood to clot at a cut?

(A)   Ⓐ

(B)   Ⓑ

(C)   Ⓒ

(D)   Ⓓ

8 Which cells are likely to engulf bacteria?

(A)   Ⓐ

(B)   Ⓑ

(C)   Ⓒ

(D)   Ⓓ

9 The MAIN function of red blood cells is to

(A) carry oxygen to body cells   Ⓐ

(B) fight disease   Ⓑ

(C) transport heat to body cells   Ⓒ

(D) carry carbon dioxide away from body cells   Ⓓ

Items **10–11** refer to the following diagram of a section through the human heart.

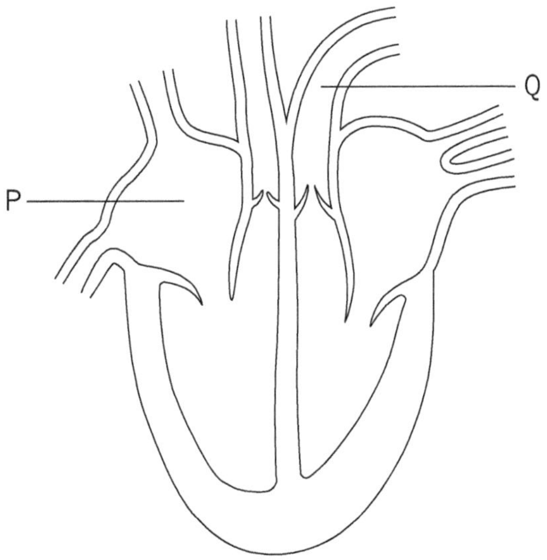

10 Chamber P is the

(A) right atrium   Ⓐ

(B) right ventricle   Ⓑ

(C) left atrium   Ⓒ

(D) left ventricle   Ⓓ

11 Blood vessel Q transports blood

(A) from the lungs Ⓐ

(B) to the lungs Ⓑ

(C) from the body Ⓒ

(D) to the body Ⓓ

12 The following events occur during one complete heartbeat.

K   The ventricles contract.

L   The atria and ventricles relax.

M   The bicuspid and tricuspid valves close.

N   The atria contract.

The correct order of events is

(A) K, L, M, N Ⓐ

(B) L, N, K, M Ⓑ

(C) N, K, L, M Ⓒ

(D) L, K, M, N Ⓓ

13 During one complete circuit around the body, a red blood cell passes through the heart

(A) once Ⓐ

(B) twice Ⓑ

(C) three times Ⓒ

(D) four times Ⓓ

14 Which option correctly matches the blood vessel and its associated organ?

	Blood vessel	Associated organ	
(A)	pulmonary artery	kidneys	Ⓐ
(B)	renal vein	lungs	Ⓑ
(C)	hepatic artery	liver	Ⓒ
(D)	carotid artery	intestines	Ⓓ

15 Which of the following blood groups is known as the universal blood donor?

(A) AB+ Ⓐ

(B) AB− Ⓑ

(C) O+ Ⓒ

(D) O− Ⓓ

16 A man with Type A Rh-negative blood

 I has antigen A on the surface of his red blood cells

 II has anti-A antibodies in his plasma

 III has the Rh factor on the surface of his red blood cells

(A) I only Ⓐ

(B) II only Ⓑ

(C) I and III only Ⓒ

(D) I, II and III Ⓓ

17 Which of the following statements is INCORRECT?

(A) The Rh factor poses a risk to a woman with Rh-positive blood who wishes to have children. Ⓐ

(B) When handling blood for transfusion, medical gloves must be worn. Ⓑ

(C) A person with anaemia should not donate blood. Ⓒ

(D) Blood must be screened for pathogens before being donated. Ⓓ

18 Which of the following factors contributes to a person developing cardiovascular disease?

(A) A low sodium diet.   Ⓐ

(B) Regular physical exercise.   Ⓑ

(C) A diet high in fat.   Ⓒ

(D) Having low blood pressure.   Ⓓ

19 Atherosclerosis can lead to

    I a heart attack

    II obesity

    III a stroke

(A) I only   Ⓐ

(B) II only   Ⓑ

(C) I and III only   Ⓒ

(D) I, II and III   Ⓓ

20 Which of the following is/are important in developing immunity to a disease?

    I platelets

    II lymphocytes

    III phagocytes

(A) I only   Ⓐ

(B) II only   Ⓑ

(C) II and III only   Ⓒ

(D) I, II and III   Ⓓ

21 Which of the following is LEAST likely to occur when a person is vaccinated against a disease?

(A) The person's lymphocytes make antibodies against the antigens. Ⓐ

(B) The person remains healthy when an outbreak of the disease occurs. Ⓑ

(C) The person develops lymphocyte memory cells. Ⓒ

(D) The person develops the disease. Ⓓ

22 Which statements given below are correct?

    I Natural immunity results from being vaccinated.

    II AIDS results from the body's immune system being damaged.

    III HIV is known as a retrovirus.

    IV The presence of foreign antibodies in a person's blood sets up an immune response.

(A) I and IV only Ⓐ

(B) II and III only Ⓑ

(C) I, II and III only Ⓒ

(D) II, III and IV only Ⓓ

23 Which of the following is NOT a social or economic effect of drug abuse?

(A) Increased demands on health services. Ⓐ

(B) Increased crime. Ⓑ

(C) Greater personal neglect. Ⓒ

(D) Lengthened life spans. Ⓓ

24 Which of the following is correct?

(A) Taking drugs of any kind is illegal. Ⓐ

(B) Cocaine can cause feelings of power and confidence. Ⓑ

(C) A person cannot become addicted to pain killers. Ⓒ

(D) Alcohol stimulates the central nervous system. Ⓓ

25 Blood doping involves

    (A) increasing the number of white blood cells in the bloodstream   (A)

    (B) decreasing the number of white blood cells in the bloodstream   (B)

    (C) increasing the number of red blood cells in the bloodstream   (C)

    (D) decreasing the number of red blood cells in the bloodstream   (D)

26 The following statements are correct EXCEPT

    (A) A person will lose weight if energy input from food exceeds energy output from daily activities.   (A)

    (B) Exercise increases the efficiency of gaseous exchange.   (B)

    (C) Muscle strength is increased by exercise.   (C)

    (D) If energy output from daily activities is less than energy input from food, a person will gain weight.   (D)

<u>Items **27–28**</u> refer to the following diagram of the human skeleton.

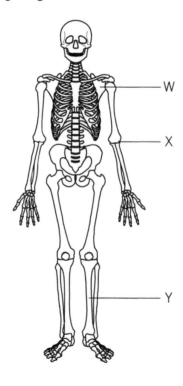

27 Which option correctly identifies the bones labelled W and Y?

	W	Y
(A)	scapula	tibia	Ⓐ
(B)	clavicle	tibia	Ⓑ
(C)	clavicle	fibula	Ⓒ
(D)	scapula	fibula	Ⓓ

28 The joint labelled X is

(A) a ball and socket joint   Ⓐ

(B) a fixed joint   Ⓑ

(C) a partially moveable joint   Ⓒ

(D) a hinge joint   Ⓓ

29 Which of the following INCORRECTLY matches a part of the human skeleton with its function?

	Part of the skeleton	Function
(A)	vertebral column	protection	Ⓐ
(B)	pelvis	manufacture of red blood cells	Ⓑ
(C)	ribs	support	Ⓒ
(D)	hind limbs	movement	Ⓓ

30 Muscles that work in opposition to cause movement of a joint are described as

(A) antagonistic muscles   Ⓐ

(B) protagonistic muscles   Ⓑ

(C) antipodal muscles   Ⓒ

(D) opposite muscles   Ⓓ

Item **31** refers to the following simplified diagram of a human forelimb.

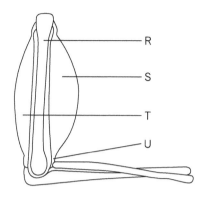

31 Which of the following is the extensor?

(A) R (A)

(B) S (B)

(C) T (C)

(D) U (D)

32 Which of the following combinations is correct when the human elbow is bent?

	Flexor muscle	Extensor muscle	
(A)	contracted	contracted	(A)
(B)	contracted	relaxed	(B)
(C)	relaxed	relaxed	(C)
(D)	relaxed	contracted	(D)

33 Which of the following statements about muscle tone is INCORRECT?

(A) Good muscle tone is important because it helps to maintain balance. (A)

(B) Exercise improves muscle tone. (B)

(C) A good upright posture is maintained by good muscle tone. (C)

(D) When resting, muscle tone maintains muscles in a relaxed state. (D)

Items **1–3** refer to the following diagram of the human respiratory system.

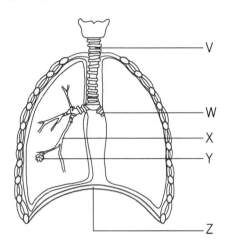

1 The structure labelled W is

(**A**) the trachea   Ⓐ

(**B**) a bronchiole   Ⓑ

(**C**) a bronchus   Ⓒ

(**D**) the larynx   Ⓓ

2 Which structure is the site of gaseous exchange?

(**A**) V   Ⓐ

(**B**) W   Ⓑ

(**C**) X   Ⓒ

(**D**) Y   Ⓓ

3 When Z relaxes it causes air to flow

(**A**) into the lungs, because air pressure in the thoracic cavity is decreased   Ⓐ

(**B**) into the lungs, because air pressure in the thoracic cavity is increased   Ⓑ

(**C**) out of the lungs, because air pressure in the thoracic cavity is decreased   Ⓒ

(**D**) out of the lungs, because air pressure in the thoracic cavity is increased   Ⓓ

4 Which option correctly summarises the pathway of air during inhalation?

(A) trachea $\longrightarrow$ bronchioles $\longrightarrow$ bronchi $\longrightarrow$ alveoli   Ⓐ

(B) alveoli $\longrightarrow$ bronchi $\longrightarrow$ bronchioles $\longrightarrow$ trachea   Ⓑ

(C) trachea $\longrightarrow$ bronchi $\longrightarrow$ bronchioles $\longrightarrow$ alveoli   Ⓒ

(D) alveoli $\longrightarrow$ bronchioles $\longrightarrow$ bronchi $\longrightarrow$ trachea   Ⓓ

5 Inhaled air contains

(A) less carbon dioxide than exhaled air   Ⓐ

(B) less oxygen than exhaled air   Ⓑ

(C) more carbon dioxide than exhaled air   Ⓒ

(D) more nitrogen than exhaled air   Ⓓ

6 Which of the following statements is true?

(A) Oxygen diffuses out of leaves during the day and the night.   Ⓐ

(B) Carbon dioxide diffuses into leaves through stomata.   Ⓑ

(C) Oxygen diffuses out of leaves through their upper surface only.   Ⓒ

(D) Carbon dioxide diffuses into leaves only during the night.   Ⓓ

7 Which of the following is/are characteristics of respiratory surfaces in both plants and humans?

     I They are thin.

     II They have a rich blood supply.

     III They have a small surface area.

(A) I only   Ⓐ

(B) I and II only   Ⓑ

(C) II and III only   Ⓒ

(D) I, II and III   Ⓓ

8 Which of the following statements about respiration is INCORRECT?

(A) Respiration occurs in all living cells. Ⓐ

(B) Respiration is the process by which body cells use energy. Ⓑ

(C) Respiration does not always require oxygen. Ⓒ

(D) Respiration helps organisms to maintain a constant body temperature. Ⓓ

9 Which chemical equation below MOST accurately summarises the process of aerobic respiration?

(A) $C_6H_{12}O_6 + 6O_2 \xrightarrow[\text{cytoplasm}]{\text{enzymes in}} 6CO_2 + 6H_2O + \text{energy}$ Ⓐ

(B) $C_6H_{12}O_6 + O_2 \xrightarrow[\text{mitochondria}]{\text{enzymes in}} CO_2 + H_2O + \text{energy}$ Ⓑ

(C) $C_6H_{12}O_6 + 6O_2 \xrightarrow[\text{mitochondria}]{\text{enzymes in}} 6CO_2 + 6H_2O + \text{energy}$ Ⓒ

(D) $C_6H_{12}O_6 + 6O_2 \xrightarrow[\text{cytoplasm}]{\text{enzymes in}} 6CO_2 + 12H_2O + \text{energy}$ Ⓓ

10 A certain diet contains equal masses of four different food substances: fat, protein, starch and sugar. If each substance is oxidised completely, MOST energy would be released from

(A) fat Ⓐ

(B) protein Ⓑ

(C) starch Ⓒ

(D) sugar Ⓓ

11 Which of the following comparisons is correct?

	Anaerobic respiration	Aerobic respiration	
(A)	requires oxygen	does not require oxygen	Ⓐ
(B)	carbon dioxide and ethanol are always produced	carbon dioxide and water are always produced	Ⓑ
(C)	very little energy is released from each glucose molecule	a lot of energy is released from each glucose molecule	Ⓒ
(D)	occurs in the mitochondria	occurs in the cytoplasm	Ⓓ

12 Which of the following statements is/are true?

    I Anaerobic respiration occurring in muscle cells produces lactic acid.

    II Fermentation of sugars by yeast when making wine produces ethanoic acid.

    III When making bread, bacteria produce carbon dioxide, which helps the bread to rise.

(A) I only   Ⓐ

(B) I and III only   Ⓑ

(C) II and III only   Ⓒ

(D) I, II and III   Ⓓ

13 The following contribute directly to air pollution, EXCEPT

(A) burning fossil fuels in power stations   Ⓐ

(B) volcanic eruptions   Ⓑ

(C) wild fires   Ⓒ

(D) using fertilisers in agriculture   Ⓓ

14 One of the MAIN causes of acid rain is

(A) sulfur dioxide   Ⓐ

(B) carbon dioxide   Ⓑ

(C) methane   Ⓒ

(D) carbon monoxide   Ⓓ

15 Which of the following is NOT a possible effect of air pollution?

(A) lung cancer   Ⓐ

(B) reduced plant growth   Ⓑ

(C) asthma   Ⓒ

(D) eutrophication   Ⓓ

16 The MAIN component of cigarette smoke that can cause cancer is

(A) nicotine   Ⓐ

(B) tar   Ⓑ

(C) carbon monoxide   Ⓒ

(D) formaldehyde   Ⓓ

17 Which of the following is LEAST likely to result from continued smoking of cigarettes?

(A) chronic bronchitis   Ⓐ

(B) addiction to carbon monoxide   Ⓑ

(C) emphysema   Ⓒ

(D) cancer of the mouth   Ⓓ

18 Which of the following statements about second-hand smoke is UNTRUE?

(A) Second-hand smoke comes from the lit ends of cigarettes.   Ⓐ

(B) Second-hand smoke is less toxic than mainstream smoke.   Ⓑ

(C) Second-hand smoke increases a non-smoker's risk of developing asthma.   Ⓒ

(D) The concentration of carcinogens is higher in second-hand smoke than in mainstream smoke.   Ⓓ

19 Smoke-free environments

    I contribute to decreased air quality

    II protect individuals from exposure to second-hand smoke

    III help people to stop smoking

(A) III only   Ⓐ

(B) I and II only   Ⓑ

(C) II and III only   Ⓒ

(D) I, II and III   Ⓓ

1 Removal of dietary fibre from the body in faeces is NOT considered to be excretion because

(A) dietary fibre is not harmful to body cells   Ⓐ

(B) dietary fibre is not digestible   Ⓑ

(C) dietary fibre is insoluble   Ⓒ

(D) dietary fibre is not produced by the body's metabolism   Ⓓ

2 Which option in the table below correctly matches the excretory organ with the waste that it excretes?

	Excretory organ	Waste excreted	
(A)	liver	bile pigments, salts	Ⓐ
(B)	skin	water, urea, carbon dioxide	Ⓑ
(C)	lung	carbon dioxide, water, salts	Ⓒ
(D)	kidney	urea, salts, water	Ⓓ

Items **3–5** refer to the following diagram of a kidney tubule and its blood supply.

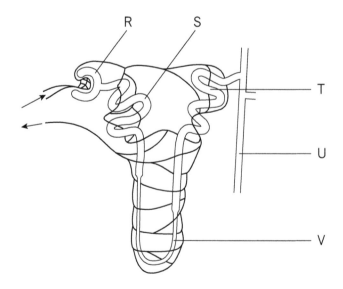

3 The structure labelled T is the

(A) first convoluted tubule   Ⓐ

(B) second convoluted tubule   Ⓑ

(C) loop of Henle   Ⓒ

(D) collecting duct   Ⓓ

4 In a healthy person, which of the following substances would be present in the filtrate in R?

(A) water, red blood cells, glucose, urea   Ⓐ

(B) glucose, salts, platelets, urea   Ⓑ

(C) amino acids, urea, salts, water   Ⓒ

(D) vitamins, water, amino acids, plasma proteins   Ⓓ

5 In which structure are amino acids reabsorbed into the blood?

(A) S   Ⓐ

(B) T   Ⓑ

(C) U   Ⓒ

(D) V   Ⓓ

6 Antidiuretic hormone causes the kidneys to

(A) produce a large volume of urine   Ⓐ

(B) reabsorb most of the water from the filtrate   Ⓑ

(C) lose a lot of water in the urine   Ⓒ

(D) reabsorb most of the salts from the filtrate   Ⓓ

7 If a healthy person drinks three large glasses of lemonade, his urine will

(A) contain glucose   Ⓐ

(B) become very dilute   Ⓑ

(C) contain very little water   Ⓒ

(D) become more concentrated   Ⓓ

8 A kidney dialysis machine

    I regulates the concentration of body fluids

    II removes glucose from the blood

    III removes urea from the blood

(A) III only   Ⓐ

(B) I and II only   Ⓑ

(C) I and III only   Ⓒ

(D) I, II and III   Ⓓ

9 Which structure in the human skin illustrated below excretes waste?

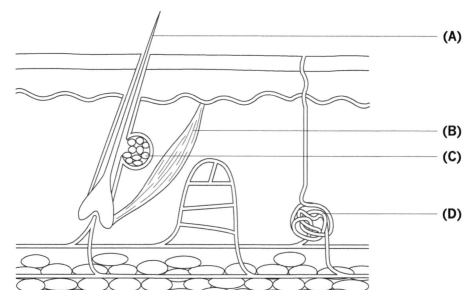

Ⓐ

Ⓑ

Ⓒ

Ⓓ

10 Which of the following options correctly summarises the events occurring in a person's skin on a very cold day?

	Arterioles	Hair erector muscles	Sweat production
(A)	constrict	contract	ceases
(B)	dilate	contract	occurs
(C)	constrict	relax	ceases
(D)	dilate	relax	occurs

Ⓐ Ⓑ Ⓒ Ⓓ

11 Which of the following lists consists of waste products of flowering plants?

(A) urea, oxygen, carbon dioxide   Ⓐ

(B) water, carbon dioxide, mineral salts   Ⓑ

(C) oxygen, water, carbon dioxide   Ⓒ

(D) mineral salts, urea, oxygen   Ⓓ

12 Waste products are lost from plants in the following ways EXCEPT

(A) active transport   Ⓐ

(B) diffusion   Ⓑ

(C) leaf fall   Ⓒ

(D) bark loss   Ⓓ

13 Which of the following would BEST enable a plant to live in dry conditions?

(A) Needle-shapes leaves with few stomata and a thin cuticle.   Ⓐ

(B) Broad leaves with few stomata and a thick cuticle.   Ⓑ

(C) Narrow, succulent leaves with few stomata and a thick cuticle.   Ⓒ

(D) Broad, succulent leaves with many stomata and a thick cuticle.   Ⓓ

1 Which option correctly matches the sense organ with a stimulus detected by it?

	Sense organ	Stimulus detected	
(A)	tongue	flavour	(A)
(B)	nose	chemicals in the air	(B)
(C)	skin	humidity	(C)
(D)	eye	sight	(D)

Items **2–3** refer to the diagram below, which shows a vertical section of the human eye.

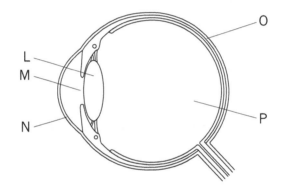

2 Structure O is the

(A) sclera   (A)

(B) iris   (B)

(C) choroid   (C)

(D) cornea   (D)

3 Which region causes the greatest refraction of light rays?

(A) L   (A)

(B) M   (B)

(C) N   (C)

(D) P   (D)

4 The image formed on the retina of the eye is

    I smaller than the object

    II inverted

    III reversed

(A) I only   (A)

(B) I and II only   (B)

(C) II and III only   (C)

(D) I, II and III   (D)

5 Which of the following options correctly identifies the events occurring when a football player walks from a sunny football field into a dimly lit changing room?

	Circular muscles of the iris	Radial muscles of the iris	Pupil	
(A)	contract	relax	dilates	(A)
(B)	relax	contract	dilates	(B)
(C)	contract	relax	constricts	(C)
(D)	relax	contract	constricts	(D)

<u>Items **6–7**</u> refer to the diagram below, which shows three different lenses in the human eye, X, Y and Z, that are adapted to view objects different distances away from the eye.

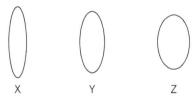

          X   Y   Z

6 Which option MOST accurately summarises the shape of a person's lenses when reading a book in their hands and then watching an aeroplane flying high in the sky?

	Reading a book	Watching an aeroplane in the sky	
(A)	X	Y	(A)
(B)	Z	X	(B)
(C)	Y	Z	(C)
(D)	Z	Y	(D)

7 The shape of lens Z is brought about by

(A) the ciliary muscles relaxing and the suspensory ligaments being pulled tight (A)

(B) the ciliary muscles relaxing and the suspensory ligaments slackening (B)

(C) the ciliary muscles contracting and the suspensory ligaments being pulled tight (C)

(D) the ciliary muscles contracting and the suspensory ligaments slackening (D)

8 Which of the following statements is INCORRECT?

(A) Objects at the far side of an opaque object cannot be seen. (A)

(B) A translucent material allows some light to pass through. (B)

(C) A narrow beam of light can be separated into its component colours by passing it through a rectangular glass block. (C)

(D) Transparent materials are see-through. (D)

9 Which option correctly compares natural and artificial light?

	Natural light	Artificial light	
(A)	it can come from kerosene lamps	it can come from light-emitting diodes (LEDs)	(A)
(B)	it does not usually contain all colours of the visible spectrum	it contains all colours of the visible spectrum	(B)
(C)	its duration cannot be controlled	its duration can be easily controlled	(C)
(D)	the intensity of it is easy to control	the intensity of it is difficult to control	(D)

Item **10** refers to the following diagram, which shows an eye with a sight defect.

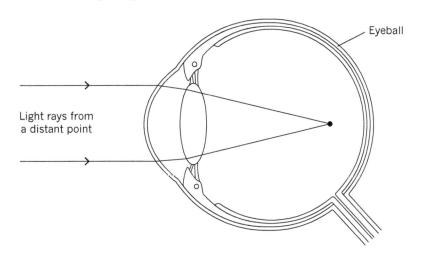

Eyeball

Light rays from
a distant point

10 Which of the following sight defects is shown?

(A) short-sightedness   Ⓐ

(B) long-sightedness   Ⓑ

(C) glaucoma   Ⓒ

(D) cataract   Ⓓ

11 Which lens, A, B, C or D, would be the BEST shape to make contact lenses for a person who is suffering from long-sightedness?

Ⓐ

Ⓑ

Ⓒ

Ⓓ

  (A)   **(B)**   **(C)**   **(D)**

12 Which of the following statements is INCORRECT?

(A) Extended exposure to ultraviolet light from the Sun can lead to cataracts.   Ⓐ

(B) Damage to the retina may lead to blindness.   Ⓑ

(C) A grain of sand in the eye can scratch the cornea.   Ⓒ

(D) Glaucoma can be treated by lens replacement.   Ⓓ

Item **13** refers to the following diagram of a human ear.

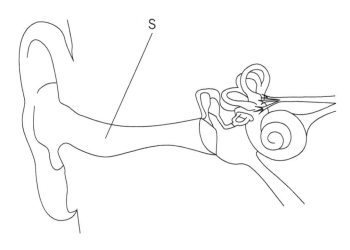

S

13 Structure S is the

(**A**) outer ear   Ⓐ

(**B**) ear canal   Ⓑ

(**C**) pinna   Ⓒ

(**D**) cochlea   Ⓓ

14 Which of the following options correctly matches the part of the ear with its function?

	Part of the ear	Function	
(**A**)	cochlea	concerned with balance	Ⓐ
(**B**)	ear drum	transmits vibrations to the ear ossicles	Ⓑ
(**C**)	pinna	collects and directs sound waves into the middle ear	Ⓒ
(**D**)	ear ossicles	transmit vibrations to the semi-circular canals	Ⓓ

15 The frequency range of sound waves detected by the human ear is approximately

(A) 2 Hz to 2000 Hz   Ⓐ

(B) 20 Hz to 20 000 Hz   Ⓑ

(C) 2 dB to 2000 dB   Ⓒ

(D) 20 dB to 20 000 dB   Ⓓ

Item **16** refers to the three sound waves illustrated by displacement vs time graphs having the same scales on their respective axes.

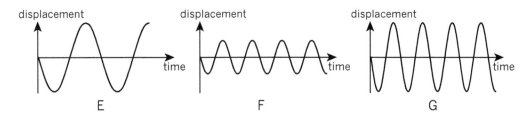

16 Which of the following statements about the sound waves is/are correct?

   I F is louder than E.

   II F has a lower pitch than G.

   III E and G have the same loudness.

(A) III only   Ⓐ

(B) I and II only   Ⓑ

(C) II and III only   Ⓒ

(D) I, II and III   Ⓓ

17 Ground staff at airports are at risk of suffering from hearing loss due to constant exposure to loud engine noise. This is MOST likely to occur because jet engines

(A) emit sounds below 20 Hz   Ⓐ

(B) emit 20 dB of sound and below   Ⓑ

(C) emit sounds above 20 000 Hz   Ⓒ

(D) emit up to 140 dB of sound   Ⓓ

Items **18–19** refer to the diagram of the human brain.

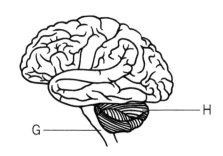

18 The structure labelled G controls

(A) conscious thought   Ⓐ

(B) posture   Ⓑ

(C) the body's internal environment   Ⓒ

(D) involuntary actions   Ⓓ

19 Structure H is the

(A) medulla oblongata   Ⓐ

(B) cerebrum   Ⓑ

(C) spinal cord   Ⓒ

(D) cerebellum   Ⓓ

20 The cerebrum of the brain controls

    I writing

    II breathing

    III memory

(A) II only   Ⓐ

(B) III only   Ⓑ

(C) I and III only   Ⓒ

(D) I, II and III   Ⓓ

Item **21** refers to the following diagram of a neurone.

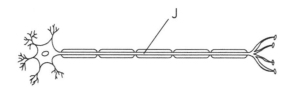

21 Structure J is

(A) an axon   (A)

(B) an axite   (B)

(C) a dendrite   (C)

(D) a dendron   (D)

22 Which of the following is/are voluntary actions?

    I sneezing

    II dropping a hot dish

    III running away from a snake

(A) III only   (A)

(B) I and II only   (B)

(C) II and III only   (C)

(D) I, II and III   (D)

23 In a simple reflex, in which order do nerve impulses pass through the reflex arc?

(A) receptor ⟶ motor neurone ⟶ relay neurone ⟶ sensory neurone ⟶ effector   (A)

(B) effector ⟶ motor neurone ⟶ relay neurone ⟶ sensory neurone ⟶ receptor   (B)

(C) effector ⟶ sensory neurone ⟶ relay neurone ⟶ motor neurone ⟶ receptor   (C)

(D) receptor ⟶ sensory neurone ⟶ relay neurone ⟶ motor neurone ⟶ effector   (D)

24 Paralysis

    I occurs when muscles are unable to relax

    II can be caused by injury to the spinal cord

    III results from messages not passing from the central nervous system to muscles

(A) I only   Ⓐ

(B) I and III only   Ⓑ

(C) II and III only   Ⓒ

(D) I, II and III   Ⓓ

Items **25–26** refer to the diagram below, which shows the positions of the main endocrine glands in the human body.

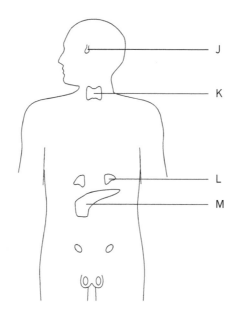

25 Structure K is the

(A) thyroid gland   Ⓐ

(B) pancreas   Ⓑ

(C) pituitary gland   Ⓒ

(D) adrenal gland   Ⓓ

26 The hormones that regulate glucose levels in the blood are produced in

(A) J   (A)

(B) K   (B)

(C) L   (C)

(D) M   (D)

Items **27–28** refer to the following hormones:

(A) antidiuretic hormone

(B) thyroxine

(C) luteinising hormone

(D) oestrogen

Match EACH item below with one of the options above. Each option may be used once, more than once or not at all.

27 A deficiency of which hormone is MOST likely to cause a person to have a slow metabolic rate?

(A)   (A)

(B)   (B)

(C)   (C)

(D)   (D)

28 Which hormone stimulates ovulation in the ovaries?

(A)   (A)

(B)   (B)

(C)   (C)

(D)   (D)

1 Which of the following is NOT a reason for maintaining good personal hygiene?

(A) It helps a person to be socially accepted. Ⓐ

(B) It helps promote good overall health. Ⓑ

(C) It helps maintain clean living areas. Ⓒ

(D) It helps to eliminate body odours. Ⓓ

2 Good personal hygiene can be maintained by

    I keeping genitals clean

    II washing hair regularly

    III once-daily washing of hands

(A) III only Ⓐ

(B) I and II only Ⓑ

(C) II and III only Ⓒ

(D) I, II and III Ⓓ

3 Which of the following is/are correct?

    I Human faeces and urine should not enter sewage systems.

    II Untreated sewage entering the environment can spread water-borne infections.

    III Uncollected garbage outside a person's home helps to increase the spread of vector-borne diseases.

(A) I only Ⓐ

(B) III only Ⓑ

(C) II and III only Ⓒ

(D) I, II and III Ⓓ

4 A plant or animal that has a harmful effect on humans, their food or their living conditions is known as a

(A) parasite   Ⓐ

(B) pest   Ⓑ

(C) vector   Ⓒ

(D) pathogen   Ⓓ

5 Which of the following is LEAST likely to encourage pests and pathogens to breed in a household?

(A) uncovered drains   Ⓐ

(B) dirty kitchen floors   Ⓑ

(C) clean toilets   Ⓒ

(D) pools of standing water   Ⓓ

6 Using fish to kill mosquito larvae is known as

(A) biological control   Ⓐ

(B) chemical control   Ⓑ

(C) mechanical control   Ⓒ

(D) sanitary control   Ⓓ

7 The diagrams show the different stages in the life cycle of a mosquito. Which is the pupal stage?

(A)   (B)   (C)   (D)

Ⓐ Ⓑ Ⓒ Ⓓ

8 The correct sequence of the stages in the life cycle of a housefly is

(A) egg $\longrightarrow$ pupa $\longrightarrow$ larva $\longrightarrow$ adult   Ⓐ

(B) adult $\longrightarrow$ egg $\longrightarrow$ pupa $\longrightarrow$ larva   Ⓑ

(C) egg $\longrightarrow$ larva $\longrightarrow$ pupa $\longrightarrow$ adult   Ⓒ

(D) larva $\longrightarrow$ adult $\longrightarrow$ egg $\longrightarrow$ pupa   Ⓓ

9 Which of the following methods would be suitable to control mosquitoes?

    I Drain all areas of standing water.

    II Spray adults with insecticides.

    III Dispose of all garden and farmyard waste properly.

(A) I only   Ⓐ

(B) I and II only   Ⓑ

(C) II and III only   Ⓒ

(D) I, II and III   Ⓓ

10 Which of the following is LEAST likely to cause food to be contaminated by pathogens?

(A) Allowing mosquitoes to land on food.   Ⓐ

(B) Washing food in water collected from a river flowing through a town.   Ⓑ

(C) Handling food when suffering from a common cold.   Ⓒ

(D) Preparing food in an unclean kitchen.   Ⓓ

11 The BEST description of waste containing discarded personal computers, mobile phones, printers and televisions is

(A) chemical waste   Ⓐ

(B) electronic waste   Ⓑ

(C) domestic waste   Ⓒ

(D) industrial waste   Ⓓ

12 Which of the following lists consists only of substances that are biodegradable?

(A) farmyard waste, food waste, garden waste   (A)

(B) food waste, rubber, waste paper   (B)

(C) plastic, garden waste, glass   (C)

(D) waste paper, farmyard waste, iron   (D)

13 Melting used PET bottles and using the product to make plastic wood is an example of

(A) recycling   (A)

(B) reducing   (B)

(C) retaining   (C)

(D) reusing   (D)

14 The BEST way for a farmer to dispose of manure and other agricultural waste is to

(A) dump it in the nearby river   (A)

(B) burn it   (B)

(C) leave it to decompose in the corner of one of his fields   (C)

(D) turn it into biogas in an anaerobic digester   (D)

15 Which of the following is MOST likely to result from dumping increasing quantities of solid waste in open dumps around the outskirts of cities in developing countries?

(A) A decrease in the incidence of gastroenteritis.   (A)

(B) An increase in the safety of drinking water.   (B)

(C) A decrease in unpleasant odours.   (C)

(D) An increase in mosquito numbers.   (D)

1 Heat is transferred through a vacuum by the process of

(A) convection   (A)

(B) radiation   (B)

(C) condensation   (C)

(D) conduction   (D)

2 When atoms or molecules collide, they transfer energy by the process of

(A) conduction   (A)

(B) convection   (B)

(C) emission   (C)

(D) radiation   (D)

3 The process of heat transfer through a medium by the movement of particles between regions of different densities is known as

(A) conduction   (A)

(B) radiation   (B)

(C) transpiration   (C)

(D) convection   (D)

4 Which of the following is NOT true concerning thermal radiation?

(A) A hot silver surface is a better emitter of thermal radiation than a hot black surface.   (A)

(B) A cool black surface is a better absorber of thermal radiation than a cool silver surface.   (B)

(C) Workers in a freezer room wearing silver suits will stay warmer than those wearing black suits.   (C)

(D) A hot, rough surface emits more radiation than a hot, smooth surface.   (D)

5 Water at 0 °C is added to two black cans, A and B, and two silver cans, C and D, as shown in the following diagram. In which can will the water warm to the surrounding room temperature soonest?

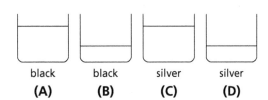

black (A) black (B) silver (C) silver (D)

Ⓐ

Ⓑ

Ⓒ

Ⓐ

6 The following diagram shows FOUR beakers of water being heated. In which beaker is the direction of the convection current/s BEST illustrated?

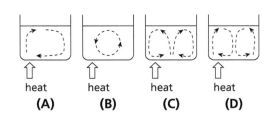

heat (A) heat (B) heat (C) heat (D)

Ⓐ

Ⓑ

Ⓒ

Ⓓ

7 In which of the following situations is heat transferred MAINLY by conduction?

(A) Being warmed by a nearby bonfire.

(B) Being warmed by hot air when looking down into an active chimney.

(C) Ironing a shirt with an electric iron.

(D) Cooking a piece of tuna in a microwave oven.

Ⓐ

Ⓑ

Ⓒ

Ⓓ

8 Which of the following is NOT true concerning a typical solar water heater?

(A) Solar energy can only reach the heater panel through the vacuum of space by radiation. (A)

(B) Solar heater panels are painted dull black so that they are good conductors of heat. (B)

(C) The storage tank is generally above the heater panel to allow for natural convection. (C)

(D) The storage tank is painted silver to reduce heat leaving it by radiation. (D)

9 The temperature in an oven is regulated by a

(A) thermometer (A)

(B) heatometer (B)

(C) thermocouple (C)

(D) thermostat (D)

Item **10** refers to the following diagram, which shows a bimetallic strip composed of brass and Invar. The left end of the strip is fixed and is attached to an insulating support.

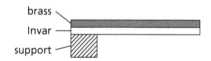

10 Brass expands more than Invar when heated. Which of the following is/are true?

 I Heating the strip causes its right end to move downwards.

 II When heated, the brass becomes hotter than the Invar, and therefore expands more.

 III Cooling the strip causes its right end to move upwards.

(A) I only (A)

(B) I and III only (B)

(C) II and III only (C)

(D) I, II and III (D)

11 During the day, coastal regions generally experience a breeze blowing in from the sea. For which of the following reasons does this occur?

(A) Cool air over the sea rises and pushes warmer air towards the coast. Ⓐ

(B) Hot air over the sea rises and pulls cooler air from the coast. Ⓑ

(C) Hot air over the land rises and cooler air from over the sea takes its place. Ⓒ

(D) Cool air over the land rises and warmer air from over the sea takes its place. Ⓓ

12 Which of the following BEST describes the temperature range of a clinical thermometer?

(A) $0\,°C \longrightarrow 100\,°C$ Ⓐ

(B) $-10\,°C \longrightarrow 110\,°C$ Ⓑ

(C) $20\,°C \longrightarrow 40\,°C$ Ⓒ

(D) $35\,°C \longrightarrow 43\,°C$ Ⓓ

13 Which of the following statements is INCORRECT in relation to a clinical liquid-in-glass thermometer?

(A) The liquid it contains can be either alcohol or mercury. Ⓐ

(B) It depends on the expansion of a heated liquid. Ⓑ

(C) Its bore has a narrow constriction. Ⓒ

(D) It is shaken so that mercury in the stem returns to the bulb for its next use. Ⓓ

14 Which of the following is true of thermometers?

(A) Thermoelectric digital thermometers cannot measure high temperatures. Ⓐ

(B) Higher temperatures can be measured by alcohol thermometers than by mercury thermometers. Ⓑ

(C) As the temperature rises in a maximum and minimum thermometer, alcohol pushes on mercury and mercury pushes on a metal index. Ⓒ

(D) Alcohol thermometers respond faster to temperature change than do mercury thermometers. Ⓓ

15 Which of the following is/are true concerning mercury and alcohol thermometers?

    I Mercury is non-toxic.

    II Alcohol must be tinted before being used in a thermometer.

    III Lower temperatures can be measured by alcohol thermometers than by mercury thermometers.

(**A**) I only   Ⓐ

(**B**) I and II only   Ⓑ

(**C**) II and III only   Ⓒ

(**D**) III only   Ⓓ

<u>Item **16**</u> refers to the maximum and minimum thermometer shown in the diagram below.

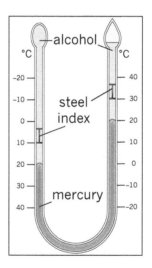

16 What have been the lowest and highest temperatures reached during the period of measurement?

	Lowest temperature/°C	Highest temperature/°C	
(**A**)	20	30	Ⓐ
(**B**)	10	30	Ⓑ
(**C**)	10	20	Ⓒ
(**D**)	20	20	Ⓓ

17 The process of water leaving a puddle and entering the air above it is known as

(A) respiration   Ⓐ

(B) evaporation   Ⓑ

(C) ventilation   Ⓒ

(D) condensation   Ⓓ

18 What will cause a wet towel to dry faster?

(A) folding the towel   Ⓐ

(B) decreased humidity   Ⓑ

(C) decreased temperature   Ⓒ

(D) decreased wind   Ⓓ

19 What type of atmosphere would cause a person to perspire MOST?

(A) warm and dry   Ⓐ

(B) warm and humid   Ⓑ

(C) hot and humid   Ⓒ

(D) hot and dry   Ⓓ

20 Which of the following is/are true concerning metabolic rate?

    I Metabolic rate is a measure of the amount of energy per unit time used by the body.

    II The temperature of a performing athlete rises as his or her metabolic rate increases.

    III Metabolic rate is a measure of the rate of chemical reactions occurring in the body.

(A) I only   Ⓐ

(B) I and II only   Ⓑ

(C) II and III only   Ⓒ

(D) I, II and III   Ⓓ

21 The process by which clean air is intentionally provided to a space and stale air is removed from it is known as

(A) respiration ⓐ

(B) evaporation ⓑ

(C) ventilation ⓒ

(D) condensation ⓓ

22 Which of the following is/are true concerning ventilation?

    I Microorganisms such as mould rapidly multiply in cold, dry environments.

    II Adequate ventilation restores the oxygen and carbon dioxide in the air to suitable levels.

    III Opening windows on opposite sides of a room can improve ventilation.

    IV An enclosed room packed with many people will become very dry.

(A) I only ⓐ

(B) II and III only ⓑ

(C) III and IV only ⓒ

(D) I, III and IV ⓓ

23 Which of the following is true concerning humidity?

(A) High humidity generally prevents the decay of wooden structures. ⓐ

(B) Air conditioners cause the air in a room to become less humid. ⓑ

(C) Humidifiers can dehydrate mucous membranes in the nose and throat. ⓒ

(D) High humidity prevents athletes from obtaining a heat stroke. ⓓ

1 The unit of energy is the

(A) joule   Ⓐ

(B) ampere   Ⓑ

(C) watt   Ⓒ

(D) volt   Ⓓ

2 Which of the following is NOT true of energy?

(A) Energy is the ability to do work.   Ⓐ

(B) Energy can be calculated from the following equation:
energy = force × velocity.   Ⓑ

(C) Energy can be transformed from one type to another.   Ⓒ

(D) Whenever work is done, an equal amount of energy is converted.   Ⓓ

3 Ajani pushes a block of weight 20 N horizontally through 5 m by applying to it a horizontal force of 10 N. The energy he uses is

(A) 2 W   Ⓐ

(B) 4 W   Ⓑ

(C) 50 J   Ⓒ

(D) 100 J   Ⓓ

4 Which of the following energy conversion sequences is/are correct?

    I Battery-operated torch light: chemical $\longrightarrow$ electrical $\longrightarrow$ heat and light

    II Photosynthesis: chemical $\longrightarrow$ light

    III Hydroelectric power station: gravitational potential $\longrightarrow$ kinetic $\longrightarrow$ electrical

(A) I and II only   Ⓐ

(B) I and III only   Ⓑ

(C) II and III only   Ⓒ

(D) I, II and III   Ⓓ

5 Which of the following statements is true? The internal combustion engine

(A) burns a mixture of nuclear fuels   Ⓐ

(B) produces harmful exhaust gases   Ⓑ

(C) is used by very few vehicles   Ⓒ

(D) prevents atmospheric pollution   Ⓓ

6 Which of the following statements is INCORRECT in relation to energy production?

(A) A biogas generator converts energy by burning coal.   Ⓐ

(B) A hydroelectric power plant converts the energy of rapidly flowing water.   Ⓑ

(C) A nuclear power plant converts the energy of a nuclear fission reaction.   Ⓒ

(D) Geothermal energy can be obtained from geysers in volcanic regions.   Ⓓ

Item 7 refers to the following diagram, which illustrates the MAIN energy conversions that occur as an aircraft takes off.

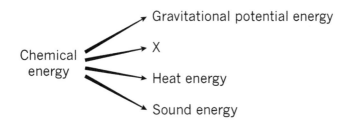

7 What type of energy is X?

(A) geothermal energy   (A)

(B) light energy   (B)

(C) electrical energy   (C)

(D) kinetic energy   (D)

8 Which of the following is/are true of nuclear fission and nuclear fusion reactions?

    I Energy is converted to mass during nuclear fission and nuclear fusion.

    II Energy is obtained from the Sun due to nuclear fusion.

    III Energy is released in nuclear power plants by the process of nuclear fission.

(A) I only   (A)

(B) I and II only   (B)

(C) II and III only   (C)

(D) I, II and III   (D)

9 Which of the following statements about energy is true?

(A) X-rays are not a form of electromagnetic energy.   (A)

(B) Sound waves are a form of electromagnetic energy.   (B)

(C) A swinging cricket bat transfers chemical energy to a ball on striking it.   (C)

(D) Energy can be transported or transferred from one point to a next by conduction, collision, convection or by waves.   (D)

Item **10** refers to the following diagram which shows wave energy incident on a concave reflecting surface.

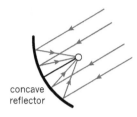

concave
reflector

10 Which of the following pairs of devices can BOTH be represented by this diagram?

(A) solar cooker / radio wave receiver (A)

(B) car headlamp / rear-view mirror (B)

(C) rear-view mirror / radio wave transmitter (C)

(D) car headlamp / radio wave receiver (D)

11 Which of the following statements concerning energy is INCORRECT?

(A) Potential energy is a stored form of energy. (A)

(B) A body possesses kinetic energy due to its motion. (B)

(C) Light waves and seismic waves are forms of electromagnetic energy. (C)

(D) Sound energy transfers through the air as vibrations. (D)

12 Which of the following can be used to calculate the momentum of a body?

(A) momentum = mass × acceleration (A)

(B) momentum = mass × velocity (B)

(C) momentum = energy × time (C)

(D) momentum = $\dfrac{\text{energy}}{\text{time}}$ (D)

13 For a collision between two objects, which of the following must be the same, before and after the collision?

(A) their total kinetic energy   Ⓐ

(B) the energy of each object   Ⓑ

(C) their total momentum   Ⓒ

(D) the momentum of each object   Ⓓ

Items **14–15** refer to a toy car of mass 8 kg which travels at a speed of 4 m s^{-1} and collides with another toy car of mass 8 kg which is initially at rest. After the collision the two cars are stuck together.

14 The total momentum before the collision is

(A) 4 kg m s^{-1} Ⓐ

(B) 8 kg m s^{-1} Ⓑ

(C) 16 kg m s^{-1} Ⓒ

(D) 32 kg m s^{-1} Ⓓ

15 The speed of the cars after the collision is

(A) 16 m s^{-1} Ⓐ

(B) 8 m s^{-1} Ⓑ

(C) 4 m s^{-1} Ⓒ

(D) 2 m s^{-1} Ⓓ

B3: Electricity and Lighting

1 Which of the following groups contains only ONE electrical conductor?

(A) plastic, copper, sea water   Ⓐ

(B) iron, wood, polystyrene   Ⓑ

(C) mercury, paper, tap water   Ⓒ

(D) rubber, graphite (a form of carbon), aluminium   Ⓓ

2 Which of the following is/are true about the uses of electrical conductors, semiconductors and insulators?

      I Semiconductors are used in the manufacture of electronic components.

      II Graphite is unsuitable for providing 'make and break' contacts in electrical circuits.

      III Copper and aluminium are used to make conducting electrical wires.

(A) I only   Ⓐ

(B) I and III only   Ⓑ

(C) II and III only   Ⓒ

(D) I, II and III   Ⓓ

Item **3** refers to the following electrical circuit, which a student has designed in order to determine the resistance of a resistor R.

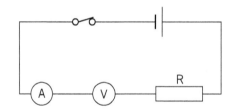

3 What is INCORRECT about the circuit shown?

(A) The ammeter should be in parallel with the resistor.   Ⓐ

(B) The voltmeter should be in parallel with the switch.   Ⓑ

(C) Both the ammeter and the voltmeter should be in parallel with the resistor.   Ⓒ

(D) The voltmeter should be in parallel with the resistor.   Ⓓ

Items **4–5** refer to the same electrical circuit described below.

A current of 2 A flows through a resistor for a period of 5 s when a voltage of 12 V exists across it.

4 The resistance of the resistor is

(A) 6 Ω (A)

(B) 10 Ω (B)

(C) 24 Ω (C)

(D) 60 Ω (D)

5 The power consumed by the resistor is

(A) 6 W   (A)

(B) 10 W   (B)

(C) 24 W   (C)

(D) 60 W   (D)

6 A lamp consumes a power of 60 W when a voltage of 120 V is placed across it. The energy it consumes in 5 minutes is

(A) 12 J   (A)

(B) 600 J   (B)

(C) 7200 J   (C)

(D) 18 000 J   (D)

<u>Item 7</u> refers to the three electrical circuits shown below having resistors connected in series and in parallel.

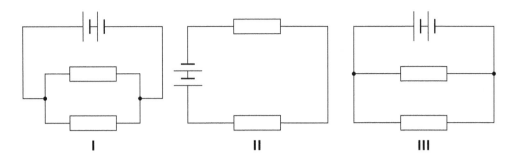

7 Which of the circuits show resistors connected in parallel?

(A) I and II only   Ⓐ

(B) I and III only   Ⓑ

(C) II and III only   Ⓒ

(D) I, II and III   Ⓓ

8 Which of the following statements is INCORRECT concerning the properties of series and parallel connections in electrical circuits?

(A) The current through components in series remains constant.   Ⓐ

(B) The sum of the currents through the branches of a parallel section of a circuit is equal to the current entering the branch point.   Ⓑ

(C) The current through each branch of a parallel section of a circuit must be the same.   Ⓒ

(D) The voltage across components connected in parallel is the same.   Ⓓ

Item **9** refers to the following electrical circuit.

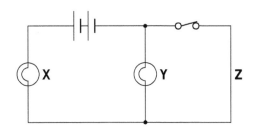

9 Which bulb/s, if any, will be lit when the switch is closed as shown?

(A) X only   Ⓐ

(B) Y only   Ⓑ

(C) X and Y   Ⓒ

(D) Neither X nor Y   Ⓓ

10 Given the voltage (V), power (P), current (I), resistance (R), energy (E) and time (t), which of the following equations is INCORRECT?

(A) $P = V \times I$ Ⓐ

(B) $V = I \times R$ Ⓑ

(C) $R = P \times V$ Ⓒ

(D) $P = \dfrac{E}{t}$ Ⓓ

11 Which of the following is INCORRECT concerning fuses used in electrical circuits?

(A) Fuses prevent excessive currents from destroying a device.   Ⓐ

(B) Fuses must be placed in parallel with a device.   Ⓑ

(C) A fuse is a short wire that can melt and thereby break a circuit.   Ⓒ

(D) The current rating of a fuse is slightly higher than the normal operating current of the device to which it is connected.   Ⓓ

12 A device is labelled as 12 V, 48 W, 50 Hz. The current rating of the fuse that should be used with the device is

(A) 3 A   Ⓐ

(B) 5 A   Ⓑ

(C) 13 A   Ⓒ

(D) 20 A   Ⓓ

13 Which of the following is correct concerning fuses and earth wires?

	FUSE		EARTH WIRE	
	Protects user	Protects device	Protects user	Protects device
(A)	✓	✓	✓	✓
(B)	✗	✓	✗	✓
(C)	✗	✓	✓	✗
(D)	✓	✗	✗	✓

14 Circuits that require high currents can overheat. To prevent overheating, these wires should be

(A) slightly insulated   Ⓐ

(B) made of poor conducting material   Ⓑ

(C) narrow   Ⓒ

(D) thick   Ⓓ

15 Which of the following devices will use the highest rate of energy?

(A) radio   Ⓐ

(B) cell phone   Ⓑ

(C) electric kettle   Ⓒ

(D) computer   Ⓓ

16 THREE 200 W televisions are used for 4 hours each day. How much energy, in kW h of electricity, is used in ONE week?

(A) $\dfrac{3 \times 200 \times 4 \times 7}{1000}$ kW h   Ⓐ

(B) $\dfrac{3 \times 200 \times 4 \times 1000}{7}$ kW h   Ⓑ

(C) $\dfrac{3 \times 200 \times 7}{1000 \times 4}$ kW h   Ⓒ

(D) $\dfrac{200 \times 4 \times 7}{1000 \times 3}$ kW h   Ⓓ

17 If the cost of electricity is 50 cents per kW h, the total cost of using FIVE 100 W light bulbs for 8 hours is

(A) $ 2   Ⓐ

(B) $ 5   Ⓑ

(C) $ 20   Ⓒ

(D) $ 200   Ⓓ

<u>Item **18**</u> refers to the following diagram showing the dials of an analogue electricity meter.

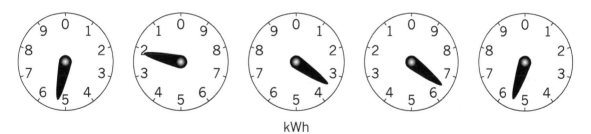

kWh

18 The reading on the meter is

(A) 53 375 kW h   Ⓐ

(B) 63 465 kW h   Ⓑ

(C) 52 365 kW h   Ⓒ

(D) 62 476 kW h   Ⓓ

19 A customer's meter reading was 25 400 kW h on 25 September and 25 900 kW h on 30 October. Electricity is charged at $ 0.50 per kW h and there is a fixed charge for the period of $ 10. The total billed for the period is

(A) $ 250   Ⓐ

(B) $ 260   Ⓑ

(C) $ 500   Ⓒ

(D) $ 510   Ⓓ

20 Which of the following practices will reduce energy consumption in the home?

    I Use of outdoor clothes lines instead of electric clothes dryers.

    II Washing only full loads in the washing machine.

    III Adjusting the heat supplied to a saucepan to the minimum required to maintain boiling.

(A) I only   Ⓐ

(B) I and II only   Ⓑ

(C) II and III only   Ⓒ

(D) I, II and III   Ⓓ

Items **21–22** refer to various types of lighting.

21 Which of the following is true of light-emitting diodes (LEDs), fluorescent tubes and filament lamps?

(A) Fluorescent tubes have the longest life expectancy.   Ⓐ

(B) Filament lamps waste the least energy as heat.   Ⓑ

(C) LEDs may withstand bounces, but filament lamps and fluorescent tubes break easily.   Ⓒ

(D) LED lamps are cheaper to purchase than fluorescent tubes and filament lamps.   Ⓓ

22 Fluorescent tubes

      I provide more efficient lighting than filament lamps and LEDs

      II cast sharp shadows

      III contain mercury, a toxic substance

      IV flicker with age

(A) I and II only   Ⓐ

(B) II and III only   Ⓑ

(C) II and IV only   Ⓒ

(D) III and IV only   Ⓓ

23 The first step to be carried out when responding to a victim who has received a severe electrical shock is to

(A) call for emergency medical help   Ⓐ

(B) remove the victim from the electrical supply using an insulated object   Ⓑ

(C) disconnect the electrical supply if the switch is nearby   Ⓒ

(D) provide CPR   Ⓓ

24 Which of the following is NOT recommended in the treatment of burns?

(A) Removing clothing that is not stuck to the burn.   Ⓐ

(B) Applying icepacks to the affected area.   Ⓑ

(C) Cleaning the wound with a mild soap and soothing with aloe vera.   Ⓒ

(D) Soaking the affected area in cool running water.   Ⓓ

25 Mouth-to-mouth resuscitation should be applied to a victim when he or she

(A) becomes unconscious   Ⓐ

(B) is in shock   Ⓑ

(C) becomes dizzy   Ⓒ

(D) stops breathing   Ⓓ

26 Which of the following combinations is necessary to start and sustain a fire?

(A) heat and fuel   Ⓐ

(B) fuel and oxygen   Ⓑ

(C) fuel, oxygen and heat   Ⓒ

(D) heat, fuel and nitrogen   Ⓓ

27 For which type of fire is water a suitable extinguishing agent?

(A) fires fueled by flammable liquids such as oils, paints and spirits   Ⓐ

(B) electrical fires   Ⓑ

(C) burning metals   Ⓒ

(D) bush fires   Ⓓ

28 What is the best method of extinguishing a fire fuelled by natural gas?

(A) Turning off the gas supply.   Ⓐ

(B) Spraying carbon dioxide over it.   Ⓑ

(C) Drenching it with water.   Ⓒ

(D) Covering it with a fire blanket.   Ⓓ

29 For which type of fire is carbon dioxide a suitable extinguishing agent?

(A) electrical fire   Ⓐ

(B) burning metal   Ⓑ

(C) flammable gas fire   Ⓒ

(D) large bush fire   Ⓓ

30 Which of the following types of fire is/are paired with a suitable extinguishing agent?

	Type of fire	Extinguishing agent
I	gasoline	carbon dioxide
II	burning metals	unreactive dry powder
III	burning cooking oil	water

(A) I only

(B) I and II only

(C) II and III only

(D) III only

31 Which of the following is NOT an electrical hazard?

(A) Using equipment having a damaged power cord.

(B) Simultaneously operating several powerful appliances connected to an electrical circuit.

(C) Using an electric hair drier whilst taking a shower.

(D) Using electrically insulated boots and gloves when repairing electrical equipment.

32 Which of the following is NOT a typical use of a respirator?

(A) To filter particles such as dust and smoke from the air.

(B) To protect the nose from high temperatures.

(C) To remove harmful gases from the air.

(D) To provide clean air in environments with polluted air.

33 Which of the following workers is LEAST likely to be using the protective gear with which they are paired below?

	Worker	Protective gear
(A)	chemist	steel-tipped leather boots, apron
(B)	welder	heat-resistant gloves, dark visor
(C)	nurse	sterile gloves, apron
(D)	worker on runway at airport	earmuffs, goggles

Item **1** refers to types of levers found in parts of the mammalian skeleton shown in the diagram below.

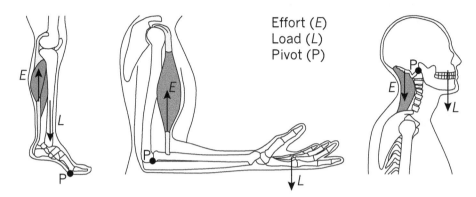

1 Which class of lever is demonstrated by each part of the skeleton?

	Foot	Arm	Head
(A)	Class 3	Class 2	Class 1
(B)	Class 2	Class 1	Class 3
(C)	Class 1	Class 3	Class 2
(D)	Class 2	Class 3	Class 1

Ⓐ
Ⓑ
Ⓒ
Ⓓ

Item **2** refers to the following diagram showing a pulley system which is assumed to be 100% efficient. An effort of 5 N is applied to the system in order to raise an object.

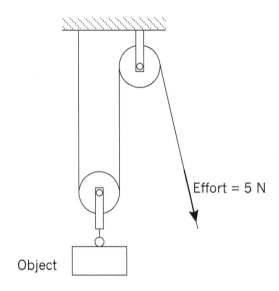

2 The weight of the object is

(A) 2.5 N   (A)

(B) 5 N   (B)

(C) 10 N   (C)

(D) 15 N   (D)

3 The diagram below shows FOUR common levers, each pivoted at a point, P. In which is the effort (E) and load (L) INCORRECTLY labelled?

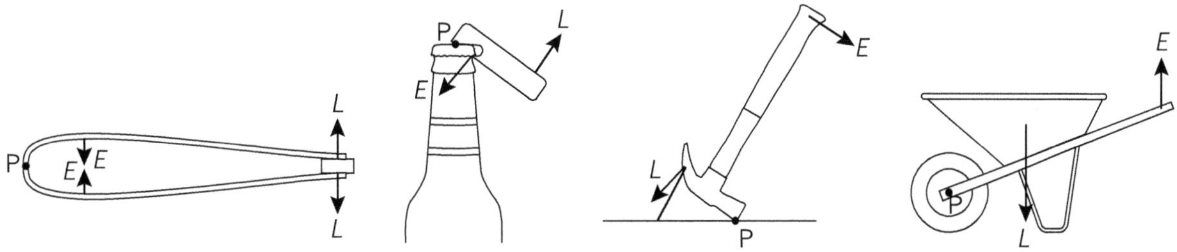

(A) Tweezers   (B) Bottle opener   (C) Hammer   (D) Wheel barrow

(A) (B) (C) (D)

4 An inclined plane is a suitable machine for

(A) raising light loads   (A)

(B) cracking nuts   (B)

(C) lifting a bucket of water from a well   (C)

(D) loading a truck with heavy objects   (D)

5 Which of the following is TRUE when using a Class 2 lever?

(A) The effort is less than the load.   (A)

(B) The effort is equal to the load.   (B)

(C) The effort is greater than the load.   (C)

(D) The effort can be the same as the load, equal to the load, or greater than the load.   (D)

6 Which of the following is TRUE of the mechanical advantage (MA) of a machine?

(A) $MA = \dfrac{effort}{load}$ (A)

(B) If the MA of machine X is greater than the MA of machine Y, then the efficiency of X is greater than the efficiency of Y.   (B)

(C) It has no unit.   (C)

(D) $MA = \dfrac{distance\ moved\ by\ load}{distance\ moved\ by\ effort}$ (D)

Items **7–8** refer to a load of 80 N being raised by a pulley system. An effort of 20 N is applied through 5 m to raise the load through 1 m during a period of 10 s.

7 The mechanical advantage of the pulley system is

(A) 0.25   (A)

(B) 4   (B)

(C) 8   (C)

(D) 16   (D)

8 The energy converted by the effort is

(A) 4 J   (A)

(B) 16 J   (B)

(C) 100 J   (C)

(D) 400 J   (D)

9 A machine is used to overcome a load by applying an effort. If it is classified as a force multiplier, then

(A) the effort is less than the load   (A)

(B) the distance moved by the effort is less than the distance moved by the load   (B)

(C) the energy input to the machine is less than the energy output from it   (C)

(D) the efficiency of the machine is greater than 100%   (D)

Item **10** refers to the following diagram, which shows a block of weight 1000 N being raised through a height of 1.2 m. An effort of 500 N is needed along the ramp of length 3 m. The efficiency of the machine is calculated as $\dfrac{\text{energy converted by load}}{\text{energy converted by effort}} \times 100\%$.

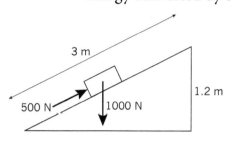

10 The efficiency is calculated as

(A) $\dfrac{1000 \times 3}{500 \times 1.2} \times 100\%$ Ⓐ

(B) $\dfrac{1000 \times 1.2}{500 \times 3} \times 100\%$ Ⓑ

(C) $\dfrac{500 \times 3}{1000 \times 1.2} \times 100\%$ Ⓒ

(D) $\dfrac{500 \times 1.2}{1000 \times 3} \times 100\%$ Ⓓ

Item **11** refers to the following diagram, which shows two cogged wheels of a bicycle linked by a chain.

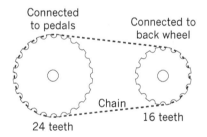

11 If the pedals are turned through two revolutions, the back wheel will rotate

(A) 3 times   Ⓐ

(B) 8 times   Ⓑ

(C) 12 times   Ⓒ

(D) 32 times   Ⓓ

<u>Item **12**</u> refers to the following diagram which shows a machine known as a hydraulic jack being used to raise a load through 1 cm by applying an effort through 20 cm.

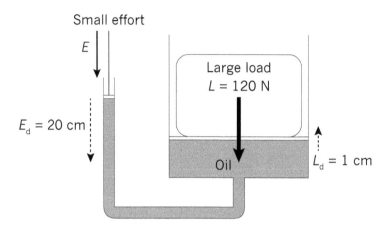

Small effort

E

E_d = 20 cm

Large load
L = 120 N

Oil

L_d = 1 cm

12 If the machine is 100% efficient, the effort (E) needed to lift the load of 120 N is

(A) 400 N   Ⓐ

(B) 800 N   Ⓑ

(C) 8 N   Ⓒ

(D) 6 N   Ⓓ

13 Which of the following will NOT lower the efficiency of a block and tackle pulley system being used to raise a load?

(A) Having to raise the load through twice the distance.   Ⓐ

(B) Increasing the weight of the lower block being raised with the load.   Ⓑ

(C) Placing sand between the pulley wheels and their axles.   Ⓒ

(D) Lubricating the surfaces of contact between the pulley wheels and their axles.   Ⓓ

1 Iron is classified as a metal because

    I it is a good conductor of electricity

    II it has a high melting point

    III it has a low tensile strength

(A) III only   Ⓐ

(B) I and II only   Ⓑ

(C) II and III only   Ⓒ

(D) I, II and III   Ⓓ

2 Which of the following options is correct?

	Metal	Use	Reason for use	
(A)	zinc	to make ornamental metal work	malleable and ductile	Ⓐ
(B)	copper	to make the bases of saucepans	good conductor of electricity	Ⓑ
(C)	tin	to coat steel cans	resistant to corrosion	Ⓒ
(D)	aluminium	to make overhead electrical cables	has a high density	Ⓓ

3 Which of the following properties suggests that rubber is a non-metallic material?

(A) It has a shiny appearance.   Ⓐ

(B) It is a good insulator.   Ⓑ

(C) It is malleable.   Ⓒ

(D) It has a high density.   Ⓓ

4 The MOST suitable material to make handles for pots and pans is

(A) wood   Ⓐ

(B) steel   Ⓑ

(C) aluminium   Ⓒ

(D) copper   Ⓓ

5 Plastics are used extensively in today's world because they

    I are durable

    II biodegrade easily

    III can be easily moulded

(A) I only   Ⓐ

(B) I and III only   Ⓑ

(C) II and III only   Ⓒ

(D) I, II and III   Ⓓ

6 Which of the following statements is NOT a reason for plastic being harmful to the environment?

(A) They are made from a renewable resource.   Ⓐ

(B) They can entangle aquatic organisms.   Ⓑ

(C) They are flammable.   Ⓒ

(D) They often release toxic chemicals when disposed of.   Ⓓ

7 Which of the following would be LEAST suitable to make high-performance sporting equipment?

(A) carbon fibre   Ⓐ

(B) kevlar   Ⓑ

(C) fibreglass   Ⓒ

(D) wood   Ⓓ

8 When the metals copper, zinc, tin and aluminium are arranged in decreasing order of reactivity, the correct order is ⓓ

(A) aluminium, zinc, tin, copper Ⓐ

(B) zinc, aluminium, copper, tin Ⓑ

(C) copper, tin, aluminium, zinc Ⓒ

(D) tin, aluminium, copper, zinc Ⓓ

9 Which of the following equations is correct?

(A) zinc + hydrochloric acid ⟶ zinc hydrochloride + hydrogen Ⓐ

(B) copper + hydrochloric acid ⟶ copper chloride + hydrogen Ⓑ

(C) tin + sulfuric acid ⟶ tin sulfate + water Ⓒ

(D) iron + sulfuric acid ⟶ iron sulfate + hydrogen Ⓓ

10 Which of the following statements about cooking utensils made from aluminium is NOT an advantage?

(A) They are good conductors of heat. Ⓐ

(B) They do not easily corrode. Ⓑ

(C) They may increase a person's chances of developing Alzheimer's. Ⓒ

(D) They are light in weight. Ⓓ

11 Alloys are often used in place of pure metals because alloys are

    I usually stronger than the pure metal

    II less likely to corrode than the pure metal

    III usually harder than the pure metal

(A) II only Ⓐ

(B) I and III only Ⓑ

(C) II and III only Ⓒ

(D) I, II and III Ⓓ

12 Brass is an alloy of

    (A) tin and copper   (A)

    (B) iron and carbon   (B)

    (C) copper and zinc   (C)

    (D) lead and tin   (D)

13 A metal usually tarnishes when its freshly polished surface reacts with

    (A) nitrogen in the air   (A)

    (B) carbon dioxide in the air   (B)

    (C) oxygen in the air   (C)

    (D) water vapour in the air   (D)

14 Which of the following metals rusts?

    (A) iron   (A)

    (B) aluminium   (B)

    (C) lead   (C)

    (D) tin   (D)

15 An experiment was set up to investigate the conditions necessary for rusting. In which tube would the nail rust the fastest?

(A)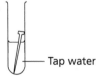
Tap water

(B)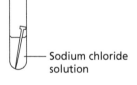
Sodium chloride solution

(A)

(B)

(C)
Oil

Boiled and cooled tap water

(D)
Calcium chloride

(C)

(D)

16 Which of the following is LEAST likely to protect a steel nail from rusting?

(A) Coating the nail with grease.   (A)

(B) Electroplating the nail.   (B)

(C) Galvanising the nail.   (C)

(D) Submerging the nail in water.   (D)

B6: Acids, Bases and Mixtures

1 Which of the following is the MOST commonly used household chemical?

(A) detergent   (A)

(B) household bleach   (B)

(C) toilet bowl cleaner   (C)

(D) water   (D)

2 Which option correctly matches the household chemical with its main chemical component?

	Household chemical	Main chemical component	
(A)	washing soda	sodium hydrogencarbonate	(A)
(B)	toilet bowl cleaner	sodium hydroxide	(B)
(C)	oven cleaner	hydrochloric acid	(C)
(D)	household bleach	sodium hypochlorite	(D)

3 Which of the following household chemicals would be BEST to use as a degreaser?

(A) Caustic soda   (A)

(B) Bicarbonate of soda   (B)

(C) Scouring powder   (C)

(D) Washing soda   (D)

<u>Items **4–5**</u> refer to the following safety symbols that may be found on some household chemicals.

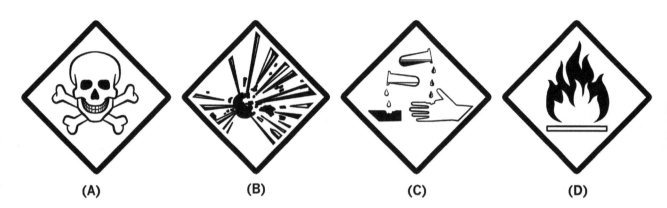

(A)   (B)   (C)   (D)

Match EACH item below with one of the options above. Each option may be used once, more than once or not at all.

4 Which symbol indicates that the household chemical is corrosive?

(A)   Ⓐ

(B)   Ⓑ

(C)   Ⓒ

(D)   Ⓓ

5 Which symbol is MOST likely to be found on a bottle of insecticide?

(A)   Ⓐ

(B)   Ⓑ

(C)   Ⓒ

(D)   Ⓓ

6 Aqueous solutions of acids

     I have a bitter taste

    II change blue litmus to red

   III are corrosive

(A) II only   (A)

(B) I and III only   (B)

(C) II and III only   (C)

(D) I, II and III   (D)

Item **7** refers to the diagram below, which shows the pH scale and the colour of universal indicator.

0	1	2	3	4	5	6	7	8	9	10	11	12	13	14
red			orange		yellow		green		blue			purple		

7 Vinegar is a weak acid, therefore it is MOST likely to turn universal indicator

(A) red   (A)

(B) yellow   (B)

(C) blue   (C)

(D) purple   (D)

8 One function of toothpaste is to neutralise any acid produced by bacteria in the mouth. To do this, toothpaste should have a pH of

(A) 1   (A)

(B) 5   (B)

(C) 7   (C)

(D) 9   (D)

9 Which option correctly classifies the household chemical named?

	Household chemical	Classification	
(A)	toilet bowl cleaner	acid	Ⓐ
(B)	household ammonia	salt	Ⓑ
(C)	chlorine bleach	acid	Ⓒ
(D)	limescale remover	base	Ⓓ

10 Which of the following statements is INCORRECT?

(A) Basic tea stains can be removed by neutralising them with borax.   Ⓐ

(B) The reaction between a base and an acid is known as a neutralisation reaction.   Ⓑ

(C) Baking soda can be used to remove acidic fruit stains.   Ⓒ

(D) Lime juice can be used to remove basic rust stains.   Ⓓ

11 Which of the following is/are true about colloids?

    I The dispersed particles never settle.

    II The dispersed particles are not visible, even with a microscope.

    III The dispersed particles are larger than those in a suspension but smaller than those in a solution.

(A) II only   Ⓐ

(B) I and II only   Ⓑ

(C) I and III only   Ⓒ

(D) I, II and III   Ⓓ

12 In which option are the household chemicals correctly classified?

	Solution	Colloid	Suspension	
(A)	household ammonia	limescale remover	metal polish	Ⓐ
(B)	window cleaner	hand cream	calamine lotion	Ⓑ
(C)	vinegar	shaving cream	liquid detergent	Ⓒ
(D)	insecticide spray	chlorine bleach	scouring powder	Ⓓ

<u>Items **13–14**</u> refer to the following apparatus.

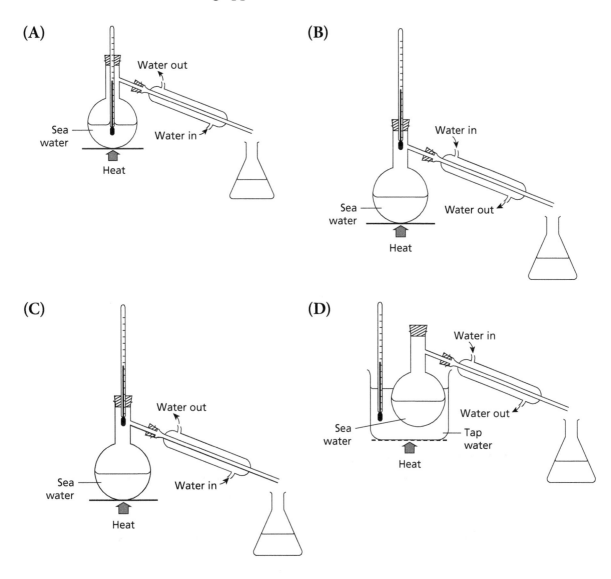

13 Which apparatus would be MOST suitable to obtain pure water from sea water?

(A)   Ⓐ

(B)   Ⓑ

(C)   Ⓒ

(D)   Ⓓ

14 The correct name of the technique illustrated is

(A) evaporation   Ⓐ

(B) condensation   Ⓑ

(C) distillation   Ⓒ

(D) solvent extraction   Ⓓ

<u>Item 15</u> refers to the following apparatus which was set up to separate sand from sea water.

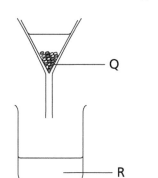

15 Which of the following correctly identifies Q and R?

	Q	R	
(A)	residue	filtrate	Ⓐ
(B)	residue	distillate	Ⓑ
(C)	filtrate	residue	Ⓒ
(D)	distillate	residue	Ⓓ

16 A forensic scientist used paper chromatography to help her identify the dyes in a sample of black ink found at a crime scene. The results shown below were obtained.

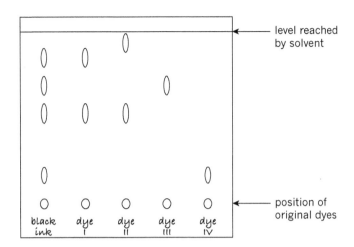

The dyes present in the black ink were

(A) I and III only (A)

(B) II and IV only (B)

(C) I, II and III only (C)

(D) I, III and IV only (D)

17 Which of the following would be BEST to remove splashes of oil paint from a tiled floor?

(A) acetone (A)

(B) turpentine (B)

(C) water (C)

(D) methylated spirits (D)

18 Which of the following statements is true?

(A) Disinfectants and antiseptics are used in the same way. (A)

(B) Disinfectants destroy microorganisms on living tissue and antiseptics destroy microorganisms on non-living objects. (B)

(C) Disinfectants are harmless to living tissue but antiseptics can irritate the skin. (C)

(D) Disinfectants destroy microorganisms on non-living objects and antiseptics destroy microorganisms on living tissue. (D)

19 Chlorine bleach must be used with care because

    I it can cause holes to appear in clothes

    II it can remove colour from clothes

    III it is acidic and can burn the skin

(A) III only   (A)

(B) I and II only   (B)

(C) I and III only   (C)

(D) I, II and III   (D)

20 Which of the following is NOT advisable when using household chemicals?

(A) Using the minimum amount of each chemical needed to ensure that the job is done properly.   (A)

(B) Following the instructions given on the label.   (B)

(C) Washing hands immediately after using each chemical.   (C)

(D) Mixing different chemicals during use to improve their efficiency.   (D)

21 Which of the following statements is INCORRECT?

(A) Oxidising agents are added to detergents to act as bleaches.   (A)

(B) Scouring powders remove dirt by acting as abrasives.   (B)

(C) Limescale removers can be used to remove calcium carbonate deposits from around taps.   (C)

(D) Rust removers are used to remove rust on aluminium appliances.   (D)

22 Which of the following options about hard and soft water is correct?

	Hard water	Soft water	
(A)	wastes soap	is good for building strong bones when drunk	Ⓐ
(B)	causes unpleasant scum to form when soap is used	does not lather easily with soap	Ⓑ
(C)	causes limescale to build up in kettles	does not contain dissolved calcium or magnesium salts	Ⓒ
(D)	lathers easily with soap	does not cause limescale to build up in hot water pipes	Ⓓ

23 The following methods can be used to soften hard water EXCEPT

(A) Boiling the water.　　　　　　　　　　　　　　　　　　Ⓐ

(B) Adding washing powder.　　　　　　　　　　　　　　　Ⓑ

(C) Distilling the water.　　　　　　　　　　　　　　　　　Ⓒ

(D) Adding sodium carbonate.　　　　　　　　　　　　　　Ⓓ

24 Which of the following occurs when a greasy shirt is washed using a soapy detergent?

(A) The hydrophilic heads of the detergent molecules dissolve in the grease.　Ⓐ

(B) The hydrophobic tails of the detergent molecules dissolve in the grease.　Ⓑ

(C) The hydrophobic heads of the detergent molecules dissolve in the water.　Ⓒ

(D) The hydrophilic tails of the detergent molecules dissolve in the water.　Ⓓ

25 Which statement is TRUE about soapless detergents but is UNTRUE about soapy detergents?

(A) The detergents remove greasy dirt from clothes.　　　　　　　　Ⓐ

(B) The detergents are made from natural fats and oils.　　　　　　　Ⓑ

(C) The detergents are often non-biodegradable and cause foam to form on rivers.　Ⓒ

(D) Scum is formed when the detergents are shaken with hard water.　Ⓓ

1 The Milky Way

    (A) is so vast that it takes light more than 100 000 years to travel across it   Ⓐ

    (B) is not a typical spiral galaxy   Ⓑ

    (C) has only two arms where the stars are concentrated   Ⓒ

    (D) has a huge black hole at its outer edge   Ⓓ

2 Outer space is the vast expanse which lies BETWEEN celestial bodies. In outer space, far from any star,

    (A) a person experiences approximately zero gravitational force   Ⓐ

    (B) objects are very hot   Ⓑ

    (C) the air pressure is like that on Earth, but the air contains no oxygen   Ⓒ

    (D) sound travels without obstruction   Ⓓ

3 Which of the following statements is/are true concerning satellites?

    I A satellite is a body that orbits another body.

    II There must be a force on a satellite directed to the centre of its curved path.

    III Geostationary, polar and GPS satellites, as well as the International Space Station, are natural satellites.

    IV Planets are satellites of the Sun and moons are satellites of planets.

    (A) I and II only   Ⓐ

    (B) II and III only   Ⓑ

    (C) II and IV only   Ⓒ

    (D) I, II and IV only   Ⓓ

4 Geostationary satellites

    I are useful in relaying TV, radio and telephone signals

    II are useful in monitoring storms

    III take 24 hours to make TWO revolutions around the Earth

    IV orbit with a radius that is greater than that of polar satellites and GPS satellites

(A) I and II only   Ⓐ

(B) II and III only   Ⓑ

(C) I, II and IV only   Ⓒ

(D) II and IV only   Ⓓ

5 Polar satellites

    I orbit the Earth directly above the equator

    II orbit the Earth several times each day

    III produce photos of lower resolution than those produced by geostationary satellites

    IV can obtain useful weather data from all around the globe

(A) I and II only   Ⓐ

(B) I and III only   Ⓑ

(C) II and III only   Ⓒ

(D) II and IV only   Ⓓ

6 Which of the following is true concerning GPS satellites?

(A) A total of 10 GPS satellites orbit the Earth.   Ⓐ

(B) They produce information of location and time at various points on or above the Earth.   Ⓑ

(C) The Hubble Space Telescope is an important GPS satellite.   Ⓒ

(D) They take 24 hours to make one revolution around the Earth.   Ⓓ

7 Which of the following lists planets of our solar system in increasing orbit radius?

(A) Mercury, Saturn, Venus, Uranus   (A)

(B) Venus, Earth, Mars, Jupiter   (B)

(C) Mercury, Mars, Uranus, Saturn   (C)

(D) Venus, Earth, Neptune, Saturn   (D)

8 Which of the following statements about the planets within our solar system is correct?

(A) They orbit the Sun in circular paths.   (A)

(B) The FOUR planets nearest to the Sun are known as the gas giants.   (B)

(C) The terrestrial planets have the lowest temperatures and no solid surface.   (C)

(D) Each of the large outer planets is orbited by a ring system of dust, or ice and dust.   (D)

Items **9–11** are about the bodies which orbit the Sun in our solar system.

9 Which of the following statements is INCORRECT?

(A) Mercury is the smallest planet.   (A)

(B) Venus is the hottest planet.   (B)

(C) All planets spin about their axes in the same direction.   (C)

(D) Jupiter is the largest planet and is orbited by the most moons.   (D)

10 Which of the following statements is correct?

(A) Neptune appears to spin on its side.   (A)

(B) The asteroid belt lies between Earth and Mars.   (B)

(C) Jupiter is known as the red planet.   (C)

(D) Saturn is known for its profound ring system.   (D)

11 Which of the following statements is/are correct?

    I Asteroids have no atmosphere.

    II Comets can produce a vapourised 'tail' of gas.

    III Meteorites are sometimes called shooting stars.

    IV Meteors are the remains of rocky materials that have fallen to the Earth.

(A) I and II only   (A)

(B) I, II and III only   (B)

(C) II and III only   (C)

(D) II, III and IV only   (D)

12 Bodies are kept in orbit around the Sun by

(A) gravitational forces   (A)

(B) frictional forces   (B)

(C) electrical forces   (C)

(D) nuclear forces   (D)

13 Which of the following is/are true concerning how Earth is affected by other celestial bodies?

    I Seasons on Earth occur because the Earth spins on a tilted axis as it orbits the Sun.

    II A lunar eclipse occurs when the Moon is positioned between the Earth and the Sun.

    III A total solar eclipse occurs on Earth where the Moon's penumbra reaches the planet.

    IV During a new moon and a full moon, the Sun, Moon and Earth are aligned.

(A) I and III only   (A)

(B) II and III only   (B)

(C) I and IV only   (C)

(D) II, III and IV only   (D)

14 We observe a new moon when the Moon appears as

(A) a complete disc of light　　　　　　　　　　　Ⓐ

(B) an obscured disc (dark disc)　　　　　　　　　Ⓑ

(C) half of a disc of light　　　　　　　　　　　　Ⓒ

(D) quarter of a disc of light　　　　　　　　　　Ⓓ

15 The period between a new moon and a full moon is APPROXIMATELY

(A) 30 days　　　　　　　　　　　　　　　　　Ⓐ

(B) 25 days　　　　　　　　　　　　　　　　　Ⓑ

(C) 20 days　　　　　　　　　　　　　　　　　Ⓒ

(D) 15 days　　　　　　　　　　　　　　　　　Ⓓ

16 Which of the following is NOT a problem of space exploration?

(A) lack of air to breathe　　　　　　　　　　　　Ⓐ

(B) sound pollution　　　　　　　　　　　　　　Ⓑ

(C) high radiation levels　　　　　　　　　　　　Ⓒ

(D) lack of gravity　　　　　　　　　　　　　　Ⓓ

17 The International Space Station (ISS)

(A) is the smallest artificial satellite put into space by humans　　Ⓐ

(B) has an orbit radius much greater than any geostationary satellite　　Ⓑ

(C) is a scientific research laboratory and an intermediate port for space exploration　　Ⓒ

(D) is owned completely by a space agency of the USA　　Ⓓ

18 Orbiters, landers, flybys and rovers are types of space probes that are used to gather information about Mars. Which of the following is NOT true of these probes?

(A) Orbiters revolve around the planet gathering information.   Ⓐ

(B) Landers drive around the planet gathering information.   Ⓑ

(C) Flybys pass very close to the planet, gather information, and then shoot off into space.   Ⓒ

(D) All space probes relay information to stations on Earth.   Ⓓ

C2: The Terrestrial Environment

1 Which of the following BEST summarises the main components of soil?

(A) air, water, minerals and microorganisms   Ⓐ

(B) rock particles, air, water and organic matter   Ⓑ

(C) plant roots, rock particles, minerals and air   Ⓒ

(D) minerals, organic matter, oxygen and water   Ⓓ

2 Which of the following contribute(s) to the formation of soil?

     I burrowing animal

     II chemical reactions

     III temperature changes

(A) I only   Ⓐ

(B) I and II only   Ⓑ

(C) II and III only   Ⓒ

(D) I, II and III   Ⓓ

3 As water freezes it can break rocks into smaller pieces by

(A) expansion   (A)

(B) melting   (B)

(C) evaporation   (C)

(D) oxidation   (D)

4 During the formation of soil, the composition of rocks is altered by

(A) chemical weathering   (A)

(B) thermal weathering   (B)

(C) physical weathering   (C)

(D) biological weathering   (D)

5 During the sedimentation test on a sample of soil, in which order will the rock particles settle?

(A) gravel, silt, sand, clay   (A)

(B) clay, silt, sand, gravel   (B)

(C) sand, gravel, clay, silt   (C)

(D) gravel, sand, silt, clay   (D)

6 Which of the following is LEAST likely to become waterlogged during the rainy season?

(A) a clay soil   (A)

(B) a silty soil   (B)

(C) loam   (C)

(D) a sandy soil   (D)

Item 7 refers to the following experiment set up to measure the volume of water retained by equal masses of three different soils. All soils were dry at the start of the experiment.

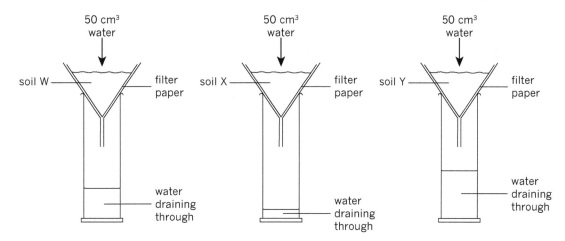

7 Which of the following options is MOST likely to be correct?

	Soil W	Soil X	Soil Y
(A)	loam	sandy	clay
(B)	clay	sandy	loam
(C)	loam	clay	sandy
(D)	clay	loam	sandy

(A)
(B)
(C)
(D)

Items 8–9 refer to the following soil profile.

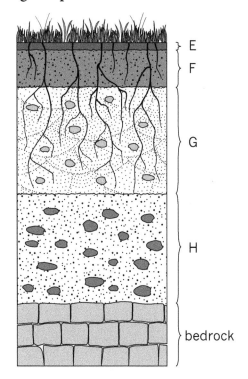

8 Which layer is known as the B horizon?

(A) E   Ⓐ

(B) F   Ⓑ

(C) G   Ⓒ

(D) H   Ⓓ

9 Which of the following statements is correct?

(A) F is called subsoil.   Ⓐ

(B) The organic matter content of F is low.   Ⓑ

(C) No living organisms would be found in G or H.   Ⓒ

(D) E contains organic matter in different stages of decomposition.   Ⓓ

10 Microorganisms decompose organic matter in the soil into

(A) clay   Ⓐ

(B) silt   Ⓑ

(C) humus   Ⓒ

(D) loam   Ⓓ

11 Organic matter is an important part of soil because it

    I converts nitrogen in soil air into nitrates for plants

    II adds mineral nutrients to the soil

    III binds fine soil particles into soil crumbs

(A) I only   Ⓐ

(B) I and III only   Ⓑ

(C) II and III only   Ⓒ

(D) I, II and III   Ⓓ

12 Which of the following is NOT a reason why earthworms are important in agricultural soils?

(A) They improve the drainage of the soil. (A)

(B) They feed on microorganisms in the soil. (B)

(C) They pull plant debris into their burrows. (C)

(D) They ingest soil particles and egest mineral-rich worm casts. (D)

13 What is soil erosion?

(A) The process by which soil is formed. (A)

(B) A process that increases soil fertility. (B)

(C) The process by which mineral nutrients are washed downwards through the soil. (C)

(D) The process by which the upper layers of the soil are worn away. (D)

14 Which of the following is MOST likely to lead to soil erosion?

(A) A lack of sunlight for three weeks. (A)

(B) Overgrazing animals. (B)

(C) Planting vegetation. (C)

(D) An unusually long dry spell. (D)

15 A farmer who wishes to reduce the loss of his soil should

    I rotate his crops

    II cover his soil with mulch

    III plough down any sloping land

(A) III only (A)

(B) I and II only (B)

(C) II and III only (C)

(D) I, II and III (D)

16 Which of the following is UNTRUE about decomposers?

(A) They are also known as saprophytes.   Ⓐ

(B) They play an important role in recycling chemical elements in nature.   Ⓑ

(C) They include bacteria, viruses and fungi.   Ⓒ

(D) They feed on waste organic matter.   Ⓓ

<u>Item 17</u> refers to the following diagram, which shows part of the carbon cycle.

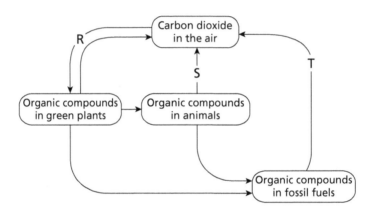

17 Which of the following correctly identifies the processes occurring at R, S and T?

	R	S	T	
(A)	photosynthesis	respiration	combustion	Ⓐ
(B)	photosynthesis	decomposition	respiration	Ⓑ
(C)	respiration	fermentation	combustion	Ⓒ
(D)	photosynthesis	respiration	decomposition	Ⓓ

18 The two MAIN processes that occur in the oxygen cycle are

(A) respiration and decomposition   Ⓐ

(B) combustion and photosynthesis   Ⓑ

(C) photosynthesis and respiration   Ⓒ

(D) decomposition and fermentation   Ⓓ

Item **19** refers to the diagram below, which shows part of the nitrogen cycle.

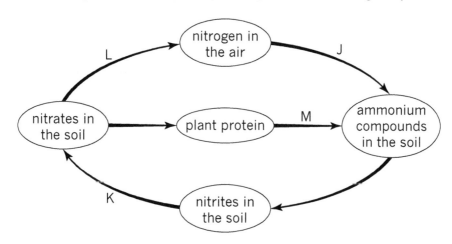

19 Which of the following statements is correct?

(A) Denitrifying bacteria carry out the process labelled J. Ⓐ

(B) The process labelled K is brought about by nitrogen-fixing bacteria. Ⓑ

(C) Nitrification is the process labelled L. Ⓒ

(D) The process labelled M is decomposition. Ⓓ

20 The correct order of events in the water cycle is

(A) evaporation, condensation, precipitation, infiltration Ⓐ

(B) condensation, precipitation, evaporation, infiltration Ⓑ

(C) precipitation, infiltration, condensation, evaporation Ⓒ

(D) evaporation, condensation, infiltration, precipitation Ⓓ

21 Which of the following air masses is correctly described?

(A) Maritime tropical: hot and dry Ⓐ

(B) Maritime polar: cool and humid Ⓑ

(C) Continental tropical: cool and dry Ⓒ

(D) Continental polar: warm and humid Ⓓ

22 Which of the following pollutants are NOT transported by air masses?

(A) industrial gases   Ⓐ

(B) landfill fumes   Ⓑ

(C) oil spills   Ⓒ

(D) particulate matter from volcanic eruptions   Ⓓ

23 Which of the following statements about air masses is INCORRECT?

(A) Cold air masses generally travel slower than warm air masses.   Ⓐ

(B) Air masses are extensive bodies of air with uniform characteristics.   Ⓑ

(C) Maritime tropical air masses occur over the Caribbean Sea.   Ⓒ

(D) Weather in the Caribbean can be affected by interactions with polar air masses.   Ⓓ

24 An occluded front is a boundary where

(A) cold air slides over warm air   Ⓐ

(B) a cold front catches up with a warm front   Ⓑ

(C) air masses of different temperatures meet but cannot displace each other   Ⓒ

(D) warm air plunges below cold air   Ⓓ

25 Which of the following types of front is INCORRECTLY paired with the weather it can produce in places where the rising air is humid?

	Type of front	Weather	
(A)	cold	vertical cumulonimbus clouds	Ⓐ
(B)	warm	horizontal stratus clouds	Ⓑ
(C)	cold	sudden, heavy rainfall	Ⓒ
(D)	warm	rainfall for a very brief period	Ⓓ

26 Which of the following fronts is paired with an INCORRECT map symbol?

(A) stationary front ▲▲◖◗ Ⓐ

(B) cold front ▼▼▼▼ Ⓑ

(C) warm front ◖◖◖◖ Ⓒ

(D) occluded front ▲◖▲◖ Ⓓ

27 Tropical cyclones

(A) originate in oceans where the temperature is below 27 °C Ⓐ

(B) have winds which deflect in a clockwise direction in the northern hemisphere Ⓑ

(C) have low pressure at their centres Ⓒ

(D) increase in wind speed as they approach land Ⓓ

28 Which of the following is/are true of hurricanes?

    I The Atlantic hurricane season is from June 1 to November 30.

    II The eyewall is a region of calm.

    III The eye is a region of strong wind and heavy rainfall.

    IV Wind direction reverses as the eye passes.

(A) I and II only Ⓐ

(B) II and III only Ⓑ

(C) II, III and IV only Ⓒ

(D) I and IV only Ⓓ

29 A tsunami

(A) is a deep-water wave Ⓐ

(B) decreases in height as it approaches land Ⓑ

(C) travels slowly but is powerful Ⓒ

(D) is produced by gravitational forces Ⓓ

30 Which of the following statements about volcanoes is NOT true?

(A) They can be formed as tectonic plates force molten rock upwards.   Ⓐ

(B) Thick lava in the vent can produce explosive eruptions.   Ⓑ

(C) Steep slopes are produced by freely flowing, non-viscous lava.   Ⓒ

(D) Gases and steam in the vent generally produce explosive eruptions.   Ⓓ

31 A lava shield volcano

(A) can spread for hundreds of kilometers   Ⓐ

(B) ejects very thick, viscous magma   Ⓑ

(C) has steep slopes   Ⓒ

(D) usually has blocked vents causing explosive eruptions   Ⓓ

32 A composite cone volcano

    I ejects rapidly flowing magma

    II ejects 'volcanic bombs'

   III has steep slopes

   IV has alternate layers of lava, and rock, ash and cinder

(A) I and II only   Ⓐ

(B) I and III only   Ⓑ

(C) II and III only   Ⓒ

(D) II, III and IV only   Ⓓ

33 Kick 'em Jenny

    (**A**) is a volcanic mountain with its peak above the surface of the Caribbean Sea Ⓐ

    (**B**) is not an active volcano Ⓑ

    (**C**) is a submarine volcano Ⓒ

    (**D**) is located just 8 km north of Dominica Ⓓ

34 Which of the following is NOT an ecological consequence of volcanoes?

    (**A**) Volcanic material usually contains useful minerals. Ⓐ

    (**B**) Land covered in lava will always be infertile. Ⓑ

    (**C**) Ash falling on the leaves of plants reduces photosynthesis. Ⓒ

    (**D**) Hot water springs of volcanic regions can be used for therapy. Ⓓ

35 Earthquakes

      I are generally produced by forces between tectonic plates

      II can have their vibrations monitored by a seismograph

      III can be compared in strength using the Richter scale; a scale of 1 to 20

      IV can cause volcanic eruptions

    (**A**) I and III only Ⓐ

    (**B**) II and III only Ⓑ

    (**C**) I, II and IV only Ⓒ

    (**D**) II and IV only Ⓓ

36 Which of the following is NOT true of tides?

    (**A**) Tides are affected by the gravitational pull of the Sun and Moon on the Earth. Ⓐ

    (**B**) A storm surge is strongest when the eye of a storm reaches the coast during a high tide. Ⓑ

    (**C**) Opposite sides of the Earth experience a high tide at the same time. Ⓒ

    (**D**) Each day, coastal regions experience one high tide and one low tide. Ⓓ

37 Which of the following is true concerning spring tides and neap tides?

(A) Spring tides occur when there is a new moon or a full moon.   Ⓐ

(B) During neap tides, high tides are very high and low tides are very low.   Ⓑ

(C) Spring tides and neap tides occur once each month.   Ⓒ

(D) Neap tides occur when the Sun, Earth and Moon are aligned.   Ⓓ

C3: Water and the Aquatic Environment

1 During a water shortage, which of the following would be the MOST important use of water?

(A) To make a jug of lemonade.   Ⓐ

(B) To wash dishes.   Ⓑ

(C) To water the garden bed.   Ⓒ

(D) To boil some potatoes.   Ⓓ

2 Water is used in agriculture

     I to grow crops hydroponically

     II to provide animals with something to drink

     III to irrigate crops

(A) I only   Ⓐ

(B) I and II only   Ⓑ

(C) I and III only   Ⓒ

(D) I, II and III   Ⓓ

3 Installing water-saving devices and appliances in the home contributes to

(A) recycling of water Ⓐ

(B) water restoration Ⓑ

(C) water conservation Ⓒ

(D) purification of water Ⓓ

4 Hydroelectric power plants

(A) boil water and use the steam to generate electricity Ⓐ

(B) generate electricity using the potential energy of moving water Ⓑ

(C) use water as a fuel to generate electricity Ⓒ

(D) use the kinetic energy of flowing water to generate electricity Ⓓ

Item 5 refers to the flow diagram below, which shows some of the processes used in the large-scale treatment of water.

screening ──────▶ sedimentation ──────▶ X ──────▶ chlorination

5 X represents

(A) precipitation Ⓐ

(B) filtration Ⓑ

(C) flocculation Ⓒ

(D) distillation Ⓓ

6 Which of the following methods would be the LEAST effective way to purify water in the home?

(A) Adding alum to the water. Ⓐ

(B) Adding chlorine tablets to the water. Ⓑ

(C) Distilling the water. Ⓒ

(D) Boiling the water for 15 minutes. Ⓓ

7 The process by which salts are removed from seawater to make fresh water for domestic use is known as

(A) desalting   Ⓐ

(B) filtration   Ⓑ

(C) desalination   Ⓒ

(D) evaporation   Ⓓ

8 Ice floats on water because

(A) the volume of ice is less than the volume of the water from which it forms   Ⓐ

(B) the density of water is higher than the density of the ice that forms from it   Ⓑ

(C) the volume of water is higher than the volume of the ice that forms from it   Ⓒ

(D) ice has a higher density than the water from which it forms   Ⓓ

9 Which of the following statements is INCORRECT?

(A) Very few substances can dissolve in water.   Ⓐ

(B) Pure water has a pH of 7.   Ⓑ

(C) Very few aquatic organisms can survive in both seawater and fresh water.   Ⓒ

(D) Pure water has a boiling point of 100 °C.   Ⓓ

10 Which of the following statements is/are correct?

    I Seawater has a lower boiling point than fresh water.

    II Fresh water has a lower melting point than seawater.

    III Seawater has a higher density than fresh water.

(A) I only   Ⓐ

(B) III only   Ⓑ

(C) II and III only   Ⓒ

(D) I, II and III   Ⓓ

Item **11** refers to the diagram below, which shows a measuring cylinder containing a liquid before and after a small stone is immersed in it. The mass of the measuring cylinder and the liquid is 140 g. When the stone is added, the total mass becomes 200 g.

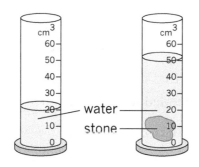

11 The density of the stone is

(A) 2 g cm^{-3} Ⓐ

(B) 4 g cm^{-3} Ⓑ

(C) 7 g cm^{-3} Ⓒ

(D) 60 g cm^{-3} Ⓓ

12 Which of the following is true of an object that FLOATS at the surface of water in a bowl?

(A) The weight of the object is equal to the weight of water in the bowl.   Ⓐ

(B) The weight of water displaced is slightly greater than the weight of the object.   Ⓑ

(C) The weight of the object is slightly less than the upthrust of the water on it.   Ⓒ

(D) The density of the object is less than or equal to the density of the water.   Ⓓ

13 A solid iron ball and an air-filled beach ball of the SAME DIAMETER are submerged in water. On releasing them, the beach ball instantly rushes upwards and the iron ball sinks. The upthrust

(A) is greater on the beach ball   Ⓐ

(B) is greater on the iron ball   Ⓑ

(C) is the same on each ball   Ⓒ

(D) on the beach ball is less than its weight   Ⓓ

14 A ship, loaded at a seaport in Trinidad, travels to a seaport in the cooler waters of the North Atlantic. Which of the following is/are true of the ship?

   I It should be loaded so that it sinks to a maximum depth indicated by the Plimsoll line recommended for loading in the waters of the North Atlantic.

   II It sinks further as it enters cooler water.

   III It experiences an upthrust equal to the weight of water it displaces.

   IV Its weight is equal to the weight of water it displaces.

   (A) I and II only   Ⓐ

   (B) I and III only   Ⓑ

   (C) II and III only   Ⓒ

   (D) III and IV only   Ⓓ

15 Which of the following activities does NOT contribute to water pollution?

   (A) Using chemical fertilisers in agriculture.   Ⓐ

   (B) Spraying pesticides to control crop diseases.   Ⓑ

   (C) Burning fossil fuels in motor vehicles.   Ⓒ

   (D) Oil tanker accidents.   Ⓓ

16 Adding excess mineral nutrients to aquatic environments and so causing algae to grow rapidly is known as

   (A) biomagnification   Ⓐ

   (B) bioenrichment   Ⓑ

   (C) eutrophication   Ⓒ

   (D) bioaccumulation   Ⓓ

17 The harmful effects of oil spills in aquatic environments include

     I coating sea birds

     II preventing oxygen from dissolving

     III smothering plants in intertidal zones

(A) I only   Ⓐ

(B) I and II only   Ⓑ

(C) II and III only   Ⓒ

(D) I, II and III   Ⓓ

18 Which of the following methods catches fish by surrounding them with a wall of netting?

(A) purse seining   Ⓐ

(B) trawling   Ⓑ

(C) throwing a cast net   Ⓒ

(D) dredging   Ⓓ

<u>Item **19**</u> refers to the following diagram, which shows a method of fishing.

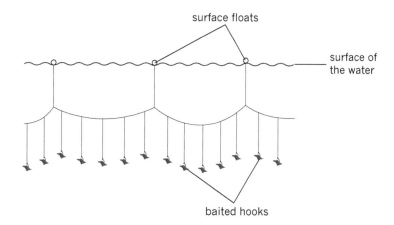

19 The method illustrated is known as

(A) long-lining   Ⓐ

(B) hook-lining   Ⓑ

(C) rod-lining   Ⓒ

(D) hand-lining   Ⓓ

Items **20–21** refer to the following navigational devices used at sea:

(A) radar

(B) magnetic compass

(C) sonar

(D) sextant

Match EACH item below with one of the options above. Each option may be used once, more than once or not at all.

20 Which device would be MOST useful on a dive boat?

(A)   (A)

(B)   (B)

(C)   (C)

(D)   (D)

21 Which device sweeps a narrow beam of electromagnetic waves around the surface of the water between a ship and the horizon?

(A)   (A)

(B)   (B)

(C)   (C)

(D)   (D)

22 The navigational device that uses satellites to pinpoint a vessel's exact location at sea is known as

(A) GDS   (A)

(B) GPS   (B)

(C) GST   (C)

(D) GSP   (D)

23 Which of the following is NOT a water safety device?

(A) an inflatable tube Ⓐ

(B) a life raft Ⓑ

(C) a life jacket Ⓒ

(D) an inflatable ball Ⓓ

24 The increase in pressure experienced by a diver as he descends has the GREATEST effect on his

(A) eyes Ⓐ

(B) ears Ⓑ

(C) nose Ⓒ

(D) tongue Ⓓ

25 A diver may develop 'the bends' if she

(A) descends for a long, deep dive too quickly Ⓐ

(B) holds her breath as she ascends Ⓑ

(C) ascends from a long, deep dive too quickly Ⓒ

(D) runs out of air as she nears the surface during her ascent Ⓓ

26 The effect similar to that of drinking alcohol that a diver feels when he dives too deeply is known as

(A) nitrogen sickness Ⓐ

(B) gas embolism Ⓑ

(C) decompression sickness Ⓒ

(D) nitrogen narcosis Ⓓ

C4: Fossil Fuels and Alternative Sources of Energy

1 An example of a fossil fuel is

(A) coal (A)

(B) biomass (B)

(C) uranium (C)

(D) wood (D)

2 A fossil fuel is used to produce electricity in a

(A) photovoltaic solar panel (A)

(B) geothermal energy plant (B)

(C) wind generator (C)

(D) diesel-electric power plant (D)

3 A non-renewable source of energy is

(A) solar (A)

(B) nuclear (B)

(C) wind (C)

(D) tidal (D)

4 For which of the following reasons is wood a renewable source of energy?

(A) It contains carbon. (A)

(B) We can never use the extremely large number of trees present on Earth. (B)

(C) It is not a fossil fuel. (C)

(D) Trees can be replanted to replace the ones we use. (D)

5 An alternative source of energy is one that is

(A) not a fossil fuel   (A)

(B) non-renewable   (B)

(C) easily replaced   (C)

(D) comprised mainly of hydrogen and carbon   (D)

6 Which of the following is an alternative source of energy?

(A) coal   (A)

(B) biogas   (B)

(C) natural gas   (C)

(D) crude oil and its distillates (e.g. diesel, kerosene and gasoline)   (D)

7 Which of the following is/are true concerning the greenhouse effect?

    I Oxygen and nitrogen are not greenhouse gases.

    II Water vapour, carbon dioxide and methane are greenhouse gases.

    III Using internal combustion engines decreases the greenhouse effect.

    IV Radiation emitted by greenhouse gases causes global warming.

(A) I and II only   (A)

(B) II and III only   (B)

(C) II and IV only   (C)

(D) I, II and IV only   (D)

8 Which of the following statements about 'acid rain' is INCORRECT?

(A) It is produced by oxides of carbon, sulfur and nitrogen dissolving in rain water.   (A)

(B) It increases as fossil fuels are burnt.   (B)

(C) It improves the nutrients in the soil.   (C)

(D) It corrodes metallic objects.   (D)

9 A student has prepared the following table, which shows emissions obtained by the burning of fossil fuels together with the effects they may produce. Which effect is INCORRECTLY paired with its emission?

	Emission	Effect
(A)	carbon monoxide	increases the ability of the blood to transport oxygen
(B)	carbon dioxide	contributes to global warming
(C)	particulate matter	reduces photosynthesis by blocking light
(D)	sulfur dioxide and nitrogen oxides	irritate the throat and lungs

Ⓐ Ⓑ Ⓒ Ⓓ

10 Which of the following BEST describes alternative sources of energy?

(A) They always require minimum capital to set up the plant. Ⓐ

(B) They always have high operational costs. Ⓑ

(C) They are generally renewable. Ⓒ

(D) They never produce negative effects on the environment. Ⓓ

11 Which of the following is NOT true of biofuels (biomass)?

(A) Biodiesel is produced from vegetable oils and animal oils/fats. Ⓐ

(B) Biogas is produced from the decay of organic matter in the absence of oxygen. Ⓑ

(C) Biofuels can only be produced from plant matter. Ⓒ

(D) Gasohol is a mixture of gasoline and ethanol produced from crops such as sugar cane. Ⓓ

12 Photovoltaic panels convert

    (A) heat energy to chemical energy   Ⓐ

    (B) light energy to heat energy   Ⓑ

    (C) chemical energy to electrical energy   Ⓒ

    (D) light energy to electrical energy   Ⓓ

13 A geothermal energy plant uses thermal energy from

    (A) solar radiation   Ⓐ

    (B) heated rocks below the Earth's surface   Ⓑ

    (C) nuclear fission reactors   Ⓒ

    (D) burning wood   Ⓓ

14 The intensity of solar energy reaching the Earth is greater

    (A) at high latitudes than at low latitudes   Ⓐ

    (B) at the tops of mountains than at their bases   Ⓑ

    (C) in clouded regions than in cloudless regions   Ⓒ

    (D) in zones with atmospheric pollution from factories than in pollution-free zones   Ⓓ

15 The use of alternative sources of energy in the Caribbean has been hindered by

    (A) the lack of availability of solar, wind and geothermal energy   Ⓐ

    (B) the heat emitted by active volcanoes   Ⓑ

    (C) the lack of funds to build the energy plants   Ⓒ

    (D) the possibility that they may cause climate change   Ⓓ

1 The following diagrams show an inflated balloon from which the air is being released. In accordance with Newton's third law of motion, the air exerts a force F_{AB} on the balloon and the balloon exerts a force F_{BA}, of equal strength, on the air.

In which of the diagrams are the forces, F_{AB} and F_{BA}, correctly labelled?

Ⓐ
Ⓑ
Ⓒ
Ⓓ

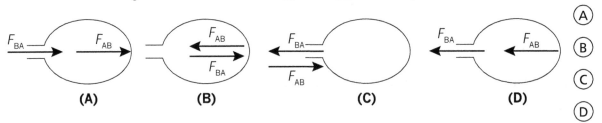

(A)　　　　　(B)　　　　　(C)　　　　　(D)

<u>Item 2</u> refers to the following diagram, which shows the air flow across the wing of an aeroplane in motion.

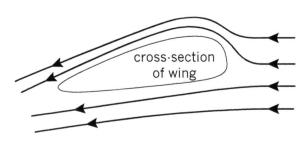

cross-section of wing

2 Which of the following is/are true?

    I The pressure above the wing is greater than the pressure below the wing.

    II There is streamlined air flow across the wing.

    III The air flow produces a resultant downward force on the wing.

    IV Birds have a similar air flow across their wings.

(A) I and II only   Ⓐ

(B) I and IV only   Ⓑ

(C) II and III only   Ⓒ

(D) II and IV only   Ⓓ

3 Which of the following is NOT true of the gravitational force on a body due to a planet?

(A) It is known as its weight. Ⓐ

(B) It is greater on a body of greater mass. Ⓑ

(C) It decreases on a body as it is submerged from air into water. Ⓒ

(D) The further a satellite is from the Earth, the less is the gravitational force on it. Ⓓ

<u>Item **4**</u> refers to the following diagram which shows an aircraft moving at CONSTANT velocity under the actions of its engine thrust, the frictional drag force, its weight and the lift force.

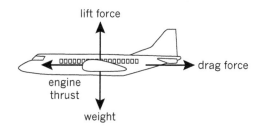

4 Which of the following pairs of conditions must be true of the magnitudes of these forces?

(A)	engine thrust = weight	drag force < lift force	Ⓐ
(B)	engine thrust = drag force	weight = lift force	Ⓑ
(C)	weight = drag force	engine thrust = lift force	Ⓒ
(D)	weight = lift force	engine thrust > drag force	Ⓓ

5 The weight of a body always appears to act through

(A) its centre of gravity Ⓐ

(B) its geometric centre Ⓑ

(C) its widest section Ⓒ

(D) its narrowest section Ⓓ

6 Which of the following pairs of conditions both increase the stability of an object?

(A) Raising its centre of gravity and increasing the width of its base.   Ⓐ

(B) Lowering its centre of gravity and increasing the width of its base.   Ⓑ

(C) Raising its centre of gravity and decreasing the width of its base.   Ⓒ

(D) Lowering its centre of gravity and decreasing the width of its base.   Ⓓ

7 The following diagram shows objects resting on flat or curved surfaces. In which is the state of equilibrium correctly labelled?

Ⓐ Ⓑ Ⓒ Ⓓ

Neutral	Unstable	Unstable	Stable
(A)	**(B)**	**(C)**	**(D)**

8 Which of the following is NOT true of the types of forces mentioned below?

(A) A centripetal force is necessary for a body to move in a curved path.   Ⓐ

(B) The force in a stretched elastic band is known as tension.   Ⓑ

(C) Only planets can exert gravitational forces.   Ⓒ

(D) Frictional force always opposes motion.   Ⓓ

9 In which of the following situations is friction NOT useful?

(A) A pulley wheel rotating on a rusty axle.   Ⓐ

(B) A person walking across a floor.   Ⓑ

(C) A car moving around a corner.   Ⓒ

(D) An aircraft decelerating to rest on a runway.   Ⓓ

10 The conditions necessary for a body to be in equilibrium under the action of parallel forces are:

      I sum of clockwise forces = sum of anticlockwise forces

      II sum of upward moments = sum of downward moments

      III sum of forces in one direction = sum of the forces in the opposite direction

      IV sum of clockwise moments about a point = sum of anticlockwise moments about that same point

(A) I and II only   Ⓐ

(B) I and IV only   Ⓑ

(C) II and III only   Ⓒ

(D) III and IV only   Ⓓ

<u>Item **11**</u> refers to the following diagram which shows a thin rod of negligible weight being used to open a can of cocoa. An effort of 5 N is applied to the left end of the rod and causes a load (*L*) to act downwards from the lid onto the rod. Point P acts as a pivot or fulcrum. A reaction force (*R*) acts upwards on the rod from the pivot, P.

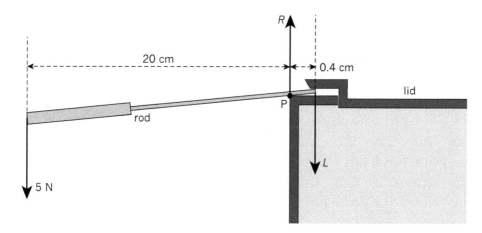

11 The value of L is

(A) 250 N   Ⓐ

(B) 100 N   Ⓑ

(C) 40 N   Ⓒ

(D) 8 N   Ⓓ

Item **12** refers to the following diagram, which shows a metre rule of weight 4 N in equilibrium (in balance) as it rests on a fulcrum. An object of weight 1 N hangs from a string at the 100 cm mark.

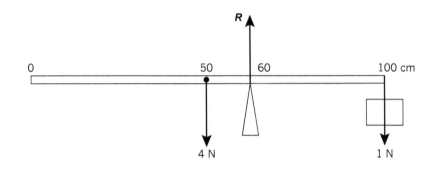

12 The upward reaction force, (R), is

(A) 1 N   Ⓐ

(B) 3 N   Ⓑ

(C) 4 N   Ⓒ

(D) 5 N   Ⓓ